WHEN WE SAY FATHER

WHEN
WE SAY
FATHER

UNLOCKING THE POWER
OF THE LORD'S PRAYER

ADRIAN ROGERS
STEVE ROGERS

PUBLISHING GROUP

NASHVILLE, TENNESSEE

978-1-4627-7130-1

Published by B&H Publishing Group
Nashville, Tennessee

Dewey Decimal Classification: 226.96
Subject Heading: PRAYER \ LORD'S
PRAYER \ JESUS CHRIST—PRAYERS

Cover design by Linda Bourdeux.

1 2 3 4 5 6 7 • 22 21 20 19 18

CONTENTS

INTRODUCTION

*"After this manner therefore pray ye: Our Father which
art in heaven, Hallowed be thy name. Thy kingdom come,
Thy will be done in earth, as it is in heaven. Give us
this day our daily bread. And forgive us our debts,
as we forgive our debtors. And lead us not into temptation,
but deliver us from evil: For thine is the kingdom,
and the power, and the glory, for ever. Amen."*
—MATTHEW 6:9–13

Our Lord has given us a model prayer. He said, *"After this
manner therefore pray ye . . ."* This is not necessarily a prayer
to be repeated by rote. Our Lord warned about vain repetitions
in this same passage. Sometimes we'll be in a public assembly and
someone will say, "Let's all stand and say the Lord's Prayer." Well,
friend, you don't say prayers; you pray prayers.

1

Suppose I come and sit down in your living room, you look at me and say, "Say a conversation." That wouldn't make much sense, would it? Prayer is not talking at God, it is talking with God. It is not rattling off beautiful thoughts, or even verses of Scripture. Jesus is giving us a model prayer. Jesus is saying, "Pray like this."

Don't try to pray for a particular length of time. It is not the length of your prayer that counts. Don't argue with God. It is not the logic of your prayer that counts. Don't use fancy language. It's not the language of your prayer that counts. It is the focus of your prayer. Focus on Almighty God. It is the force of your prayer. Pray in the power of the Holy Spirit of God. It is the faith of your prayer. Pray, believe, and you'll receive; pray and doubt, you will do without."

> *"Prayer can do anything God can do, and God can do anything."*

How important it is that we learn to pray. Friend, the time will come, if it is not already here, that for God to answer your prayer will be the most important thing to you on this earth. You can learn many things. But you can learn nothing better than to learn how to pray.

Nothing can stand against the man who can pray because prayer can do anything that God can do, and God can do anything. It has well been said that nothing lies outside the reach of prayer except that which lies outside the will of God. You do not have a need but what proper prayer would help you to attain that which you need. You do not have a failure in your life but what proper prayer would have avoided that failure. You do not have a burden, a heartache, a tear, or a fear that proper prayer cannot help to remove, to soothe, to bless, to help, to heal. I'm telling you, my dear friend, that prayer is the order of the day. The prayer Jesus taught His disciples to pray begins with these words: "Our Father." Don't just lightly pass over these two words. They are the key to the entire prayer. When we say Father, we express His nature. God is Father. When we say Father, we expect His nurture. He will take care of us. And when we say Father, we exalt His name.

God is Father. We come to Him as His children. Incredible things are in store for us "when we say Father."

CHAPTER 1

Our Father

"The Person of the Prayer"

"After this manner therefore pray ye: Our Father which art in heaven, Hallowed be thy name."

—MATTHEW 6:10

Think about prayer. Think about God being the heavenly Father, and ask yourself this question: Why do I pray? Why should I have to tell God what He already knows? Why should I ask Him for what He already wants to give?

We Do Not Pray to Instruct God

Many times our prayers are little more than a laundry list of the things we think God needs to do for us: "God, I need a job, and I need for You to work out this situation, and I've got to know if it's Your will for me to get married this year, or wait until next year."

The Bible *does* tell us *"in every thing by prayer and supplication with thanksgiving let your requests be made known unto God"* (Phil. 4:6). However, there is a big difference between bringing our needs before the Father and instructing Him. We do not pray to instruct God.

We Do Not Pray to Impress God

Sometimes we think we're impressing God by using a certain kind of rhetoric—designed to impress those who are listening. Jesus scolded the Pharisees for praying like that: *"And when you pray, you shall not be like the hypocrites. For they love to pray standing in the synagogues and on the corners of the streets, that they may be seen by men. Assuredly, I say to you, they have their reward"* (Matt. 6:5 NKJV). Jesus also told us we don't have to use a lot of liturgical lingo, repeating the same religious sounding phrases over and over: *"And when you pray, do not use vain repetitions as the heathen do. For they think that they will be heard for their many words. Therefore do not be like them"* (Matt. 6:7–8 NKJV).

That ought to be an encouragement to many of us—that we don't have to be a junior-size Shakespeare in order to pray. You may have been present at an event when someone has been asked, "Would you lead us in prayer?" "Oh," came the reply, "I can't pray." Well, now wait a minute. Can he talk? If he's a child, can he talk to an earthly father? If an earthly child can talk to an earthly father, you can talk to your heavenly Father. You don't have to use King James English. You don't have to put some "thee's" and "thou's" into your prayer. It's all right to pray using everyday language. God understands modern English, and He can understand you when you pray; just speak to God out of your heart.

We Do Not Pray to Inform God

You can't tell God anything He doesn't already know. A wise man said, "Has it ever occurred to you that nothing ever occurs to God?" Nothing takes the Father by surprise; nothing catches Him off guard. God knows it all, the beginning and the end. He says in this passage of Scripture, *"Your heavenly Father knows what you have need of before you ask Him" (Matt. 6:21, author paraphrase).* You don't pray to tell God something He didn't know. You don't pray to inform God.

We Pray to Invite God

Here is why we pray to God our Father—not to instruct Him, not to impress Him, not to inform Him, but to invite Him. Prayer is God's way of bonding us with our heavenly Father.

A while back, I was invited to speak at a college. I said, "I'm sorry. I would like to come, but I just can't. My schedule will not allow it." They said, "Please. If you'll come, we'll send a private airplane over and pick you up." I said, "All right. I'll go." When the plane came to pick me up, it was an airplane with only two seats— one for the pilot, and the other for me. The pilot said, "Pastor, can you fly?" I said, "No." He said, "Would you like to fly this airplane?" I said, "Sure." He said, "Take the controls. It's yours."

You need to get the mental picture: he's sitting right next to me, telling me what to do, but my hands are on the controls, flying the airplane. It was great fun, and I enjoyed doing something I'd never done before. Of course, when it came time to land, I had relinquished the controls back to the pilot. Taking off is optional; landing is mandatory. Now here's the whole point. He could fly it without me; I could not fly it without him. But he allowed me to fly it with him, and we were having wonderful fellowship.

In the same way, God can do it without us; we cannot do it without Him, but God allows us to do it with Him. And the way He allows us to do it with Him is by prayer. By that prayer, we have a bonding with God, a fellowship with God, and we can know God, not just as the great ruler of the universe, but we can know God as our heavenly Father.

I'd like you to think with me about three things that happen when we pray, when we say Father:

When We Say Father, We Express God's Nature

What is God's nature? God is Father. Throughout history, the philosophers have had all kinds of ways that they talk about God. Aristotle called God "the unmoved mover." In other words, to Aristotle, prayer doesn't affect God at all. Huxley called Him "the eternal unknown." Arnold called Him "the absolute unknown." The generation that has grown up watching *Star Wars* might want to refer to Him as "the Force"—some sort of mysterious energy field in the ether out there that moves and controls things. And if you talk to the man on the street, when he speaks of God, he'll speak of Him perhaps flippantly, irreverently as "the man upstairs."

But who is God? Jesus taught us to call Him Father. Pay close attention. One hundred and sixty-seven times in the Bible, Jesus called Him Father. Do you think that's by happenstance? No. God is Father to us. Now there are those today who think that God is not Father, and that perhaps we ought to call God Mother.

The following article appeared in the *Wall Street Journal*, April 27, 1992:

The Lord's Name: Image of God as "He" Loses Its Sovereignty in America's Churches

More worshipers challenge language that describes the Supreme Being as male

LONG BEACH, CA. The First Congregational Church here looks every inch a bastion of religious tradition. Inside the imposing Italian renaissance structure graced with delicate rose windows are mahogany pews and a grand old pipe organ. Then the Sunday service begins. "May the God who mothers us all bear us on the breath of dawn, make us to shine like the sun, and hold us in the palm of her hand," intones Mary Ellen Kilsby, the pastor.

A number of theologians warn that language shapes reality. And unless the church changes its imagery, it will effectively endorse gender and race bias. By insisting on God as Father, they say, traditionalists risk deifying a mere word, committing the sin of idolatry.

The Reverend Kilsby's preaching has encouraged her congregation toward eclecticism. And, as they gather over coffee after Sunday service, members talk about how they picture God: as a cloud, a formless spirit, mother earth.

What conclusion are we left with? If you insist on using the Bible word *Father*, then you have "deified" a word; you are an idolater. Now that's slick, isn't it? So anybody who insists on calling God Father is an idolater. Jesus, when He taught us to pray Father, what was He doing? He was expressing gender and race bias. We ought to be ashamed of Jesus.

In reality, when we call God Father, we are not just merely attributing to God human attributes, and making God in our image. Father is not what God is like; Father is what God is. Someone may ask, "Is God a man?" Of course not! God is not a man; God is not a woman. God is Spirit. But God is Father. And when we call God Father, we're not talking biology; we're talking theology. It's very important that you understand this, because if you don't understand it, your knowledge of the Bible is going to be all skewed.

Divine Fatherhood is not a reflection of human fatherhood. It is not that since we are fathers, we project that onto God, but to the contrary. All human fatherhood is patterned after the divine Fatherhood. Father is what God is.

That brings up a problem, because some have been raised by fathers who were harsh or neglectful or dishonest or cruel or maybe absent, and we ask, "That's what a father is like? God is like my father? Then maybe I don't want to have much to do with Him."

We can't look at a human father, and infer that's what God must be like. On the other hand, every human father ought to endeavor to be more like God. First Corinthians 8:6: *"But to us there is but one God, the Father, of whom are all things, and we in him; and one Lord Jesus Christ, by whom are all things, and we by him."* But to us there is one God, the Father.

Some people ask me, "Do you believe that Allah is God?" Of course not! They reply, "Well, the Muslim believes in one God, and we believe in one God, so we all believe in the same God." That's ridiculous. What if we were to agree that Tennessee has one capital, but I say it's Nashville, and you say it's Memphis. However, we say, "Isn't that wonderful? We all believe in one capital." Things that are different are not the same. The one God, the true God is the Father of our Lord Jesus Christ. He is the triune God.

Where Is God?

When the model prayer says, *"Our Father, which art in heaven,"* what is it talking about? Is it talking about the abode of God where the saints who have graduated to glory are? Actually, this means "in the heavenlies," in the spiritual realm. It means that God is everywhere. There is no place where your Father is not. Therefore, your Father is not an absentee Father; He's always with you. A wise man said, "God is a circle whose center is everywhere and whose circumference is nowhere." There is no place where God is not. He is our Father in the heavens. That means that He's right here with me and He's right there with you.

My wife, Joyce, and I love to walk hand in hand on the beach when the sun is setting. It's incredible. And when that sun is setting, there's a shimmering path of shining gold that comes across the ocean. And as Joyce and I are walking down the beach, that path comes right to us. But, you know the amazing thing? There may be a couple up a hundred yards ahead of us, and that path is coming right to them. And another couple a hundred yards ahead of them, and that path is coming right to them.

Everybody has God all to himself. In fact, God doesn't love us all; He loves us each. He loves every one of us. And He is our Father in the heavenlies; that is, He is here with us, not just somewhere way beyond the blue, peeking down from above the clouds. He is ever present.

When We Say Father, We Experience God's Nurture

Do you know what the word *nurture* means? Nurture means "to take care of." So many times we think of our responsibility to God, and we do have a responsibility to God, because He is our Father. But have you ever thought of God's responsibility to you?

Whenever a couple brings children into this world, they're responsible for them. If they don't take care of them, they're guilty of a crime in our society; they can be put in jail for child neglect. I want to tell you here some good news. Our heavenly Father will never be arrested for child neglect. We experience His nurture. He is the God who is going to take care of us. How does

He get to be our Father? He doesn't have the responsibility for all the people in this world. He does, as sovereign king, as judge, but not as Father.

There's a doctrine around called the Universal Fatherhood of God and the Universal Brotherhood of Man: It says this—that God is the Father of all, and we're all brothers. That sounds good, that sounds so sweet, but there's one thing wrong with it.

> *"God doesn't love us all; He loves us each."*

It's not so. He is the Creator of all of us. And in the broadest sense, with a stretch of the word, you could call Him the Father, but not in the spiritual sense. Not all people are children of God; only those who are born into His family. Jesus said in John 8:44 when He was speaking to the Pharisees, *"You are of your father, the devil, and the lusts of your father ye will do . . ."*

In this world, there are some who are children of God and there are some who are sons and daughters of the devil. We don't become God's child until we're born into God's family. In John 1:12 we read: *"But as many as received him [Jesus], to them gave he the power to become the sons of God, even to them that believe on his name."* Here's another verse: *"For ye are all the children of God by faith in Christ Jesus"* (Gal. 3:26). God becomes our Father by conception, therefore, and not by creation.

Somebody will still want to argue and say, "God created all things, so that makes us His children." Well, God created rats and roaches and buzzards and rattlesnakes, but He's not their Father. God is the Father of those who have been born into His family by the Lord Jesus Christ. First Peter 1:23: *"Being born again, not of corruptible seed, but of incorruptible, by the word of God, which liveth and abideth for ever."*

We Can Expect God's Care

Since we experience His nurture, what are some things we can expect? First of all, we can expect His care. If He is our Father, He cares for us. In this same passage, Matthew 6:26, the master teacher, the Lord Jesus Christ, who taught us to call God Father, said this: *"Behold the fowls of the air: for they sow not, neither do they reap, nor gather into barns; yet your heavenly Father feedeth them. Are ye not much better than they?"*

Now, I'm my Father's child, and as His child, I don't have to beg. When our children were living at home and Joyce had prepared a wonderful meal, she didn't say to the children, "Now, kids, dinner's ready. Get down on the floor and beg and plead, and maybe I'll give you a scrap or two." No. She said, "Come, dears, dinner's ready. Help yourself." Think of the logic that Jesus is using. He's saying, "Look. If God feeds the fowls of the air, isn't your Father going to take care of you?" What farmer would feed his chickens and starve his children? That's the logic that Jesus is using. And then He says, "Therefore, take no thought what you're going to eat, what you're going to drink, what you're going to wear." What are we worried about? The big F's: food, fitness, finance, fashion. Don't worry about those things. But the point is that God has committed Himself to feed you, to take care of you.

And do you know what worry is? Worry is an insult flung into the face of God. Now suppose I come home. My little children are there. They're small. And I see them over there in the corner, sniffling and crying and whimpering. I say, "Dears, what's wrong?" "Well, Daddy, we're just afraid we're not going to have anything to eat. We're afraid we're not going to have a bed to sleep in. We're concerned, Daddy, that we won't be able to stay in our house. Daddy, we're afraid somebody's going to come in and harm us." How do you think that would make me feel as a father?

What they are saying really when they worry like that is, "Dad, you're not able to take care of us. We don't think you're going to be able to bring some food home or be able to pay the rent. We don't think that you're going to be able to protect us if somebody comes in here and tries to harm us." Now let's be real. I'm only a human. I may not be able to protect them. But do we ever have to fling such an insult into the face of God and act as though God cannot take care of us; that He's not strong enough, loving enough, good enough, kind enough, wise enough, thoughtful enough to take care of us? Worry is an insult to Almighty God. He is our Father. He is not going to be arrested for child neglect. I can expect His nurture in the realm of His care.

We Can Expect God's Correction

Because He's my Father, He's going to correct me. Notice what the master teacher, Jesus, said about the Fatherhood of God. *"For if ye forgive men their trespasses, your heavenly Father will also forgive you. But if ye forgive not men their trespasses, neither will your Father forgive your trespasses"* (Matt. 6:14–15). That is, an unforgiving spirit is unforgivable.

The Bible teaches that our Father corrects us when we do wrong. It's delineated even more clearly in Hebrews 12:5–7: *"And have ye forgotten the exhortation which speaketh unto you as unto children, My son, despise not thou the chastening of the Lord, nor faint when thou art rebuked of him: For whom the Lord loveth he chasteneth, and scourgeth every son whom he receiveth. If ye endure chastening, God dealeth with you as with sons; for what son is he whom the father chasteneth not?"*

> *"Worry is an insult flung into the face of God."*

Now if God is my Father, not only can I expect His care; I can expect His chastisement. God doesn't chastise us because He doesn't love us, but because He *does* love us. *". . . whom the father loves he chastens . . ."* Perhaps you had a father who, when he took you to the woodshed, said, "I'm just doing this because I love you; this hurts me more than it hurts you." My father said, "You know, I'm doing this, Adrian, because I love you." Well, he loved me far more than he loved my brother. I was his favorite. Why did he do that? I'm grateful now that he loved me enough to chastise me.

If you're a child of God, you can expect when you pray, "Father," that you're going to know God's nurture, and that's going to be care and it is going to be chastisement. Have you ever wondered why it seems like God's children have trouble and sometimes the devil's crowd doesn't? The writer in Psalm 73 almost lost his faith over that thing. He said, "I've been chastened all day long. And I look at these fat cats out here who don't give a hoot about anything, and they just seem to be sailing through life." You know the difference? God deals with the devil's crowd on credit; God deals with His children on cash. Do you know the difference between cash and credit?

"Charge It!"

When I was a little boy, we lived on Florida Avenue in West Palm Beach. Right up the hill was Georgia Avenue. And sitting up on the top of the hill was the community grocery store where we did our shopping. And I would go up there with my dad sometimes and watch him buy groceries.

One day, my brother and I were in there. I witnessed the most amazing thing I'd ever seen. I was just a kid now, very young. And my dad got a sackful of groceries and walked out and he said two words to that grocer. I'd never heard them before. Some incredible words. He said, "Charge it!" That's all he said. "Charge it!" And that grocer wrote something on a little pad and my dad walked out with those groceries. I said to my brother, "Did you hear that? All he said was 'charge it.'"

And so the next day we went to that grocery store. We walked in, and he knew whose kids we were. We bought some cookies and a candy bar. And then came the magic moment. We said, "Charge it!" He said, "Okay," and we walked out with that stuff. Wow! I had found the key to Fort Knox. Those were the most unbelievable two words I'd ever heard—charge it! Day after day we made our trek to Mr. Oliver up there at the community grocery store on Georgia Avenue. "Charge it!" "Charge it!" "Charge it!" One day, my daddy called us in. He had received the bill! Now, friend, I want to tell you, when you charge it, payday comes. He gave us a short course in finance that I will never ever forget. Now that's credit. Payday is coming.

Do you know what the Bible says in Romans 2:5? *"But after thy hardness and impenitent heart treasurest up unto thyself wrath against the day of wrath and the perdition of ungodly men."* What does that mean? It means you're just putting wrath in the bank. When you live as an unsaved child of God and you sin, it's just put on your account. You're just saying, "Charge it! Put it on my account." But one of these days God's going to call you in and there will be a reckoning. That reckoning is the final judgment. So people that think they're getting away with their sin are not getting away with it at all. It's all on God's record. It's all on God's ledger. And the payday is coming someday. But God doesn't deal with His children on credit; He deals with them on a cash basis. God loves you when you sin, but He loves you too much to let you stay that way. He'll carry you into the woodshed and God will chastise, not because He doesn't love you, but because He *does* love you.

Sometimes people think that when they do something wrong, God is going to cast them off. No, He's not. A little boy may go out and play in the mud and then start to go into the house, covered with mud from head to toe. His father sees him and says, "Son, you can't go in the house with all that mud on you," and he takes the hose and hoses the little kid off there in the driveway before he goes inside. It's not the boy that the father is rejecting; it's the mud. We are God's children. And thank God He still loves us—mud and all—even though sometimes He may have to hose us down. As His child, you not only can expect His care; you can expect His correction.

We Can Expect God's Compassion

The Bible says, *"Like as a father pitieth his children, so the LORD pitieth them that fear him"* (Ps. 103:13). In Matthew 6:8,

Jesus talks about the heathen and the pagans, and He says, *"Be not ye therefore like unto them: for your Father knoweth what things you have need of before ye ask him."* Your Father knows your needs. Matthew 10:29–30: *"Are not two sparrows sold for a farthing? And one of them shall not fall on the ground without your Father."* That is, your Father tends the funeral of little birds. *"But the very hairs of your head are all numbered."* That's how much He loves you.

Oh, He has His sights on you. That's the reason I said it's so easy to talk to Him. You don't have to use King James English. You don't have to use poetic expressions when you pray to God. Just talk to Him out of your heart. The Bible says in Romans 8:14–15: *"For as many as are led by the Spirit of God, they are the sons of God. For ye have not received the spirit of bondage again to fear; but have received the Spirit of adoption, whereby we cry Abba, Father."* *Abba* is an Aramaic diminutive. The closest translation we would have to that is "Daddy, Father." Have you ever thought of God as Daddy? Friend, that's not being irreverent. "God has sent forth the Spirit of His Son into our hearts, crying Abba Father." Daddy, Father.

You can be so intimate with God without understanding God. When I was a little boy, my dad sold Buick automobiles at East Coast Motors. He'd get all dressed up. And he had a little valise that he carried. He'd kiss my mother goodbye and go off to work. I didn't have any idea where my dad was going. But one thing always intrigued me. He said, "I'm going to see a party." I thought, *he gets to go to so many parties.* I had no idea what he did. But I did not have to understand what he did to know he was my abba father, that I could love him, and that he loved me. He had compassion. He knew what I had need of and cared for me.

A father was a bookkeeper back before computers. He did his work in his home office. He had a ledger. He was one of these guys—you may be like him—everything was perfect! No erasures, no smudges. Every line, every entry—just right. When he was working, he had a rule that the children weren't allowed to come in. But the door flew open and his little four-year-old son ran and jumped in his father's lap while he was sitting there at the desk, knocking his father's arm. The ink smeared right across the page. The father put the pen down and looked at him. He said, "Son, look what you've done. You've ruined it all. I told you not to come in here when I'm working." The little boy started to cry. Through his tears, he said, "Daddy, I'm sorry. I just wanted to sit in your lap and rub your beard."

When the father heard that, he was so heartbroken. He realized that his small son and that moment were far more important than his old ledger. He closed the book and put the pen down, picked the little boy up and, kissing away the tears, said, "Son, I'm so glad you came in to see me." And they went on to talk about things that a father and a son could talk about.

Friend, aren't you glad that your heavenly Father is never so busy flinging out the sun, the moon, and the stars, and running this universe, and keeping His ledger that He doesn't have time to stop and talk with you? Wherever you are, your Father desires and deserves and wants your companionship. When you say Father, you experience His nurture—His care, correction, and companionship—because we have a heavenly Father.

When We Say Father, We Exalt His Name

Right in connection with calling Him Father, He says we're to pray this way: *"Our Father, which art in heaven. Hallowed be thy name."* Oh, we have a wonderful heavenly Father, and His name is Jehovah, Yahweh. And because we have the family likeness to wear and the family loyalty to share, we have the family name to bear. When I used to take my children to school and pull up in front of the school and let them out, almost invariably I would say, "Now, children, remember who you are and whose you are. You belong to Jesus, who you are. And whose you are, you belong to me."

We Recognize His Name

And we need to recognize His name. You know what Jesus said in John 17, speaking to the Father in verse 6? *"I have manifested thy name unto the men which thou gavest me out of the world. Thine they were, and thou gavest them me, and they have kept thy word."* What was Jesus saying? He said, "I want you to know My Father's name. I want you to know His name so you can hallow it." Philippians 2:9: *"Wherefore God also hath highly exalted him*

[Jesus], and given him a name which is above every name." Is His name above the Father's name? No, He and the Father are one. And God the Son and God the Father have a name together that is to be hallowed.

We Reverence His Name

What is the name of the Father? Well, did you know that when you use the name of Jesus, you're using the Father's name? Do you know what *Jesus* means? It means Jehovah Saves. We're to recognize the name, and we are to reverence the name. "Hallowed be thy name." Never talk flippantly about the name of God. Hopefully, you would not curse and use abject, overt profanity, but the great Bible expositor G. Campbell Morgan said, "I am more concerned about the blasphemy of the sanctuary than I am the blasphemy of the street."

Did you know that God's name is used, so many times among us, irreverently? I've been with preachers when a preacher would do something silly and another preacher would say, "Bless him, Lord." Well, now if he didn't really mean that, "My God, bless him," he ought not to say it. Sometimes people win a prize and say, "O my God!" Do they really mean "O my God"?

What does it mean to take God's name in vain? It means to use God's name any way, in any form, without reverence. Never ever use God's name carelessly or flippantly. The Bible says, *"God will not hold him guiltless that taketh his name in vain"* (Exod. 20:7).

Corrie ten Boom, that great Christian lady, taught us that we're not to wrestle, but nestle with God. She taught us intimacy with God. There's not any difficulty with intimacy with God. You can call Him Daddy, but do it with the deepest respect.

We Rely Upon His Name

Not only do we recognize the name and reverence the name, but because He is Father, we rely upon His name. John 14:13–14: *"And whatsoever ye shall ask in my name, that will I do, that the Father may be glorified in the Son. If ye shall ask any thing in my name, I will do it."* And once we see that God has done it, how we need to give Him the praise and the honor and the glory. I've seen God answer prayers in my life—small prayers, big prayers. I want my children to know that God is a prayer-answering God.

Years ago, our family was getting ready to take a vacation to Florida. There was a man in our church who had a brand-new luxury motor home. He said, "Adrian, I want you to take this motor home when you take your family vacation." I said, "Oh, that's wonderful. That's going to be so great." We all loaded up and got in the motor home and drove to a condo on the ocean that we had rented in Satellite Beach. On Sunday we decided to go to church in Titusville where my friend Peter Lord pastored— about thirty miles from where we were. After we got back to the condo on Sunday afternoon, I got out of the motor home and looked and one of the hubcaps on the rear wheel of that great big motor home was missing.

Now that hubcap was bigger than a garbage can lid. Shiny, all chrome. It would cost a king's ransom to buy another one. And the motor home looked like somebody with a tooth knocked out, you know. It was terrible. I thought, *Oh no, we've lost a hubcap*. I did not want to take that motor home back unless it was in pristine condition because that's the way I got it. I said to my boys, "Boys, let's go look for that hubcap."

Our trip to church that morning had been about thirty miles, and a lot of it was just through raw, open country. And I thought, *Well, maybe if we just drive along and look carefully, we might see it along the roadside.* So we drove about twelve or fifteen miles, out in the middle of nowhere and stopped at random; I mean just stopped at random and got out. And I said, "You boys just walk along the road here and look."

And I thought to myself, *You know, this is so foolish.* But before we had gone, I'd gathered the boys together, and I said, "Let's pray that God will help us find that hubcap." So we prayed.

As I walked along the road, I said to the Lord, "Lord, here's what I did. I asked the boys to pray with me. And, Father, we prayed about that hubcap. Father, would You help us to find that hubcap, not so much for the hubcap, but that these boys might know that You answer prayer." That was the great desire of my heart. I just wanted them to see an answer to prayer.

Now remember, we were out in the boonies. Driving along a thirty-mile stretch of nothing, we had stopped at random. And as I was walking, I glanced down in the ditch that ran alongside the road. Lying in about four inches of water was that hubcap. I said, "Boys, come get this hubcap. Let's go home!" And they came and fished it out of the water and we took it home.

Now God doesn't always answer my prayers with that specificity, but He does it enough in my heart and in my life to let me know that these things are not always just coincidences. There's no way that could be a coincidence, no way on God's green earth. Such a small thing. But it wasn't a small thing. It wasn't the hubcap. I think it was the Father saying, "Adrian, just as you care for those boys, I care for you. I know where everything is. I know how to run this world. I am your Father."

When we say Father, we express His nature. God is Father. When we say Father, we expect His nurture. He will take care of us. And when we say Father, we ought to exalt His name. What a wonderful God we have. *Hallowed be thy name.*

CHAPTER 2

First Things First

"The Priority of the Prayer"

*"Thy kingdom come. Thy will be done
in earth, as it is in heaven."*

—Matthew 6:10

I heard some time ago about a man who saw a talking parakeet for sale. Talking parakeets are generally expensive. This one was only fifteen dollars. So he asked the store owner, "Does this parakeet truly talk?" "Certainly." "Only fifteen dollars?" "Yes." "Well, I'll take him." The store owner replied, "Now the cage, of course, is thirty dollars." The man said, "Okay, that's still not too bad. Forty-five dollars; I've got the bird and the cage."

The man was back at the pet store in several days. He said, "You know, the bird doesn't talk." The store owner said, "You did get a little swing, didn't you?" The man asked, "A swing?" "Yes," the store owner replied. "Before he talks, he has to get on the swing and swing." The man asked, "Well, how much is a swing?" "Ten dollars." "I'll take a swing, please."

The man came back again in several days. He said, "Hey, the bird has not said a word." "The store owner replied, "You mean to say that that bird got on the swing and then looked in the mirror and didn't say anything?" The man asked, "What mirror?" "Oh," the store owner exclaimed, "You didn't get a mirror? You need one of these twelve-dollar mirrors." The man said, "All right, give me a mirror."

A few days later the man was back. He said, "The bird is still not talking." The store owner said, "Oh, don't tell me. You mean the bird got on the swing and swung, and looked in the mirror, and went up and down the little ladder and didn't say a word?" The man asked, "What ladder?" The store owner replied, "You didn't get a ladder? Oh, you need one of these nine-dollar ladders."

The man bought a ladder and soon was back, same story. He said, "Mister, this bird is not saying a word." The store owner asked, "You mean to say he pecked the bell and didn't say anything?" "What do you mean?" "Oh, he always pecks the bell before he talks." "All right. I want the bell."

Then one day the man came in the pet store. He went straight to the owner and said, "Mister, that bird died!" "He died?" the owner asked. "He sure did." "Well, what happened?" "He got on the swing and he swung back and forth. And then he went up and down the little ladder. Then he came back down and he looked in the mirror. And then he pecked the bell. And then he turned to me and said something." "Oh," said the store owner, "he did talk! What did he say?" "He said, 'Don't they sell any birdseed in that store?' And then he dropped over dead!"

Something more important than the bell and the mirror and the ladder is the birdseed. In this chapter, I want to talk to you about proper priorities—putting first things first.

Here's what Jesus said in Matthew 6:10: "*Thy kingdom come. Thy will be done in earth, as it is in heaven.*" That is the priority of the prayer—for God's kingdom to come, for God's will to be done. In verses 31–33 of the same chapter we read, "*. . . What shall we eat? or What shall we drink? or Wherewithal shall we be clothed? (For after all these things do the Gentiles seek:) for your heavenly Father knoweth that ye have need of all these things. But seek ye first the kingdom of God and his righteousness; and all these things shall be added unto you.*"

What He's talking about here, therefore, in this prayer is the power of proper priorities.

Most of us get in trouble when we put God in second place and put things first. We are living in the realm of things, when, instead, we're to be, according to what Jesus taught us to pray, seeking first the kingdom of God and His righteousness. When that happens, the Bible tells us, "all these things shall be added unto us."

Is It Full?

Stephen Covey tells a story about a professor in college teaching time management to his students. He came in the class one day with a big, wide-mouth jar that would hold several gallons. He also had some big rocks, about the size of a fist. He put those rocks in the mouth of that jar until the rocks came all the way up to the top. Then he asked the students, "Is the jar full?" The students nodded their heads. He said, "No, it's not full."

Then he reached under his desk and got a bucket of gravel and poured the gravel in on top of the rocks. The gravel began to fill in around the rocks. He shook it down real good and asked, "Now is the jar full?" They were afraid to answer, but some nodded, "Yes, it's full now." He said, "No, it's not full yet." He reached under his desk and got a bucket of sand and began to pour the sand in on top of the gravel and the big rocks, and shook it and smoothed it off at the top. He said, "Now is the jar full?" They were too skittish to answer. And some of the wiser ones said, "No, it's not full yet." He said, "You're right."

And then he reached down and got a bucket of water and poured the water in the jar. As he did, it seeped down through the sand, through the gravel, and around the big rocks. It came all the way up to the brim. And he said, "Now is the jar full?" And they said, "We think so." He said, "You're right. The jar is full."

Then the professor asked, "Now what is the lesson?" Various ones of them said things like, "Well, there are a lot of lessons there. Perhaps the lesson is that you may think that you can't get any more in your life, but with proper management, you can always squeeze something else in."

He said, "No, that is not the lesson. Here is the lesson. If I had not put the big rocks in first, I never would have got them in."

Friend, what you and I need to do is determine what are the big rocks. A lot of times we are living our lives, and our jar is filled with gravel and sand and water. Then we come to the end of the trail and we find out we did not put the big rocks in first. We did not have proper priorities. And so our Lord, in this incredible lesson on prayer, teaches us that we've got to have proper priorities. *"Seek ye first the kingdom of God and his righteousness; and all these things shall be added unto you"* (Matt. 6:33).

Three basic thoughts I want to lay on your heart and etch on your consciousness, and you'll keep them forever.

The Principle of God's Preeminence

What is the kingdom of God? The kingdom of God is that realm where God is preeminent, where He is King, where He is supreme. Let me tell you something about our God. Our God will not take second place to anything or anybody. Our God is not a moonlighting God, a part-time God, and His throne is not a duplex. He demands, He desires, He deserves preeminence. He deserves first place. Colossians 1:17–18: *"And he is before all things* [speaking of Jesus], *and by him all things consist. And he is the head of the body, the church: who is the beginning, the firstborn from the dead; that in all things he might have the preeminence."*

God doesn't want a place in your life; God doesn't want prominence in your life; God demands preeminence in your life.

Dear reader, I don't know your name, but I do know something about you. It is the same thing that is true about every human who walks this planet: In every person's heart there is something that is first place. And if that is not God and His kingdom, your life is out of whack.

"God is not a part-time God, and His throne is not a duplex."

S. D. Gordon said this: "In every heart there's a throne. When self is on the throne, Christ is on the cross. When Christ is on the throne, self is on the cross." No one can serve two masters.

What is God up to? What is the mystery of history? The mystery of history is simply this: that Jesus might have preeminence.

That's What I Want Too

What is the ministry of the Holy Spirit? A lot of believers want to be filled with the Spirit. They pray, "Lord, fill me with the Spirit. I want to be a person of great of faith." God says, "Ho-hum." "Well, Lord, fill me with the Spirit. I want to live a holy life." The Holy Spirit says, "I'm not interested." "Well, Holy Spirit, fill me. I want to understand the mysteries of the Bible." The Holy Spirit says, "I couldn't care less." "Holy Spirit, fill me. I want to be a great soul winner." "Ho-hum."

Something's wrong here. Let's see if we can figure out what's wrong. "Holy Spirit, fill me. I want Jesus Christ to be glorified in my life." He says, "You do? That's what I want too. Let's get together. You want Jesus Christ to be glorified? So do I. And, by the way, I might make you a man or woman of faith. By the way, I'll help you to live a holy life. By the way, I'll help you to understand the Bible. I'll help you to win souls that Jesus might be glorified." That's God's purpose!

Jesus said, concerning the Holy Spirit, "He shall not speak of Himself. He'll not glorify Himself, but He shall speak of Me" (see John 16:13–15). I hear people talk about "the Holy Spirit, the Holy Spirit, the Holy Spirit" to such a degree that they've almost denigrated Jesus. Friend, if you ever see a parade and it seems that the Holy Spirit is leading that parade, He's not, and there's something false there. But if you see a parade and Jesus is leading the parade and the Holy Spirit is standing on the sidelines, saying, "Look at Him, look at Him," there's something real about that. Just be aware of any movement that is led by the Holy Spirit.

Do you think I'm taking away from the ministry of the Holy Spirit? Not at all. I love the dear, precious Holy Spirit. He lives in me. He dwells in me. But why is He there? That in all things Jesus might have the preeminence.

This is what made the apostle Paul the great man that he was. He had a life that was dedicated to the preeminence of Jesus. He says in Philippians 3:13: *"Brethren, I count not myself to have apprehended: but this one thing I do, forgetting those things which are behind, and reaching forth unto those things which are before, I press toward the mark for the prize of the high calling of God in Christ Jesus."*

Paul's life was narrowed to one thing. The secret of power is concentration. If you take a swamp, and narrow the water and run it over a gorge, it can run a power dam. If you take light, and concentrate it until it gets to be a laser, you can cut steel with it. Your life is going to be powerful when you can say, "This one thing I do."

Have you ever wondered why we're going to have a final judgment? That Jesus might have preeminence. There is coming a day when every knee shall bow and every tongue shall confess that Jesus Christ is Lord. That's the mystery of history. That's what God is up to. And, friend, if you want power in your life, find out what God is up to and get in on it. Give Jesus the preeminence. Seek first His kingdom and His righteousness.

A man running a race has no side issues. Watch the men and women who run in the Olympics. They've laid aside every weight. They have their eye fixed on the goal. The Bible says that a double-minded man is unstable in all of his ways. That's the reason we have to be careful that good things don't take away from the best things. The apostle Paul said in 1 Corinthians 6:12: *"All things are lawful unto me, but all things are not expedient . . ."* Paul was saying, "I'm running a race; I can't afford to get distracted."

Sometimes a Christian may have a questionable habit, and they say, "Well, what's wrong with this? Does the Bible say I can't do it? Is there a law against it?" That's not the question. Is it expedient? We don't use the word *expedient* much anymore. But there's another word that is related to expedient that helps us understand its meaning. Think of the word *expedition*. That means something that's going to carry you to a destination. An expedition is going somewhere. If a thing is not expedient, it means it doesn't bring you to your goal.

Now if you don't have any goals, thinking about whether something is expedient or not is meaningless to you. But if you have some goals, if you can say with the apostle Paul, "My goal in life is Jesus Christ, that He might have preeminence," then everything is measured by that. Some things are not bad in themselves, but you don't run a race with an overcoat on.

Suppose you have saved up enough money to go on a cruise that you've been dreaming of. Then you ask yourself, "Do I have a right to go on a cruise? Do I have a right to spend the money, to spend the time to go on a cruise?" Question: Will you be a better person for having been on a cruise or not? Will you be refreshed, renewed, relaxed, restored? Is this going to help you on your goal? Fine. God's not opposed to recreation. Recreation is what? Re-creation. Jesus said, "Come apart and rest a while."

God doesn't mind you having a wonderful meal. The same God that made the salt pork made the strawberries. Do you think He made it for the devil's crowd? God loves you. God enjoys you having a good time. But you cannot let a good time take you away from God. If you go on a cruise and come away loving God less than you did before you went, then it was not expedient to you. Seek first the kingdom of God.

> *"Some things are not bad in themselves, but you don't run a race with an overcoat on."*

Take anything and everything you do—your job, your pleasure, your friends, your family—and measure it by this standard: Is it helping me to be a better Christian?

We can ask for personal things, but never selfish things. Can you ask for a job? Yes! Can you ask for food? Yes! But seek first the kingdom of God. You may be wondering why things are not working out for you. Can you honestly say, "My desire is the kingdom of God?" Can you honestly, sincerely begin every prayer with, *"Thy kingdom come; thy will be done"*? Remember, prayer is not some way that you bend God's will to fit your will. Prayer is finding the will of God and getting in on it. And a good thing becomes a bad thing when it takes the place of the best thing. And the best thing is the kingdom of God and His righteousness.

The Practice of God's Preeminence

What does it mean to seek Him first? Here are some of the priorities required:

Give God the First Thoughts of the Day

The Bible says, *"In the morning will I direct my prayer unto thee and look up"* (Ps. 5:3). Someone wrote these words: "Every morning lean thine arms awhile upon the windowsill of heaven and gaze upon the Lord. Then with the vision in thine heart, turn strong to meet the day."

I have a little habit I'd like to share with you—I "pace" myself for the new day, using the letters P-A-C-E. It's personal with me, but I want to suggest you might try it. P stands for praise; A stands for acceptance; C stands for control; and E stands for expectation. I do this every day when I wake up.

P Stands for Praise

First of all, I praise the Lord. I lift my hands to the Lord and say, "I praise You, Lord, that You gave Yourself for me. And because, Lord, You've given Yourself for me, Your blood cleanses from all sin, and I do not have to start this day with any unconfessed sin." I can start this day brand new, for His mercies are new every morning. I don't have to drag yesterday's sin and sorrow and failure into today. "I praise You, God, that You gave Yourself for me."

A Stands for Acceptance

Then I turn my hands over like I'm receiving a gift, and say, "Lord, not only do I praise You that You gave Yourself for me, but now, Lord, I accept that You've given Yourself to me. Lord, I just receive You in all of Your fullness."

C Stands for Control

Then I put my hands up like somebody put a gun on me, and I say, "Lord, I surrender to You; I put myself under Your control. You gave Yourself for me, that You might give Yourself to me, that You might live Your life through me. General Jesus, this is Private Adrian, reporting in. I'm under Your control; I'm

Yours today; I am expendable to You, whatever You want me—as best I know how—to do, say, be, or give."

E Stands for Expectation

And then I'll spread my arms out as wide as I can, and say, "Lord, it's going to be a great day because You and I are going to live it together. This is the day the Lord has made. I will rejoice and be glad in it."

PACE—Praise. Acceptance. Control. Expectation. I encourage you to try it. By doing so, you give Him the first thoughts of the day.

Give God the First Day of the Week

Sunday is not the weekend. It certainly wasn't made for Michelob! Sunday is the Lord's Day. It is the first day of the week, and it is to be given to Him. Acts 20:7 says, *"Upon the first day of the week, when the disciples came together to break bread, Paul preached unto them . . ."* Sunday is not the Sabbath. Saturday is the Sabbath. Sunday is the Lord's Day. It is the first day of the week and we give it to Him. The Bible gives us Sabbath laws, but it doesn't tell us how to live the Lord's Day. It just tells us it's the Lord's Day. Don't get caught up in wondering, "Can I do this or that on the Lord's Day?" Instead, ask yourself these questions:

"Have I given this day to the Lord? Have I set aside the first day of the week for Him?" Start your morning right. Start your week right.

Give God the Firstfruits of Your Income

Proverbs 3:9 says, *"Honor the Lord with your possessions, and with the firstfruits of all your increase"* (NKJV). Don't eat the cake and give Him the crumbs. Don't say, "Now I've got to pay the mortgage. I've got to pay the light bill. I've got to pay Sears. I've got to pay for the groceries. And if there's anything left, I'll give it to the Lord." No! You put things before God when you do that. *"Honor the Lord . . . with the firstfruits of all your increase"* (NKJV). The next verse goes on to say, *"So your barns will be filled with plenty, and your vats will overflow with new wine"* (NKJV).

I read about a congressman who took his son out for some father-son fellowship. He let his boy choose the place, so they went to McDonald's. The boy ordered some fries. As they were talking, the dad reached over to get a french fry. The boy put his hand on his dad's hand, and said, "Dad, those are my fries." The congressman thought, "My son has an attitude problem. Doesn't he know that I bought him those fries? Doesn't he know that I could take them away from him if I wanted to? And doesn't he know I don't need his fries? If I wanted fries, I could get my own fries. And doesn't he know I have enough money in my pocket to bury him with french fries if I wanted to?"

And then he said, "God spoke to my heart and convicted me about the way I am with my stewardship. God says 'I want this.' 'Hey, hey, God, that's mine, Lord, that's mine.' God says, 'Don't you know that I'm the one who gave that to you to begin with? Where did you get it? You got it from Me. And don't you know if I wanted to, I could take it away from you at any time I want?'"

And He could, couldn't He? Do you think God needs what you have to run His universe? He doesn't! *"The earth is the LORD's, and the fullness thereof"* (Ps. 24:1). And don't you know that God could bury you with french fries, spiritually, if He wanted to?

So what do we do when we're stewards, when we give Him the firstfruits? It's just our way of recognizing who He is.

Give God the First Consideration in Every Decision

Give Him the first thought in the morning; give Him the first day of the week; give Him the firstfruits of your income. And then, give Him the first consideration in every decision.

Second Corinthians 8:5: *". . . but they first gave their own selves unto the Lord . . ."* Before you give anybody anything, give yourself to Jesus. Your choice of a job, your choice of a vocation, your choice of a mate, whatever it is, has to be made in the light of Calvary.

What would you think of a pastor of a church where his ministry is being blessed, he has a sense that he's where God wants him, and the people do too, and then another church comes along and offers him a bigger salary, and he says, "Well, folks, I'm sorry, I've got to go. This church is offering me more money than you're paying me. I've got to go." If you were a member of that church, you'd probably say, "Is that what he's in the ministry for, for money? Good riddance, let him go!"

Now here's another question: What would you think of a businessman who is involved in ministry in his church, his family is ensconced there, his children are in a Christian school, and then a business comes along and says, "Look, we're going to give you a promotion. You've got to leave Dallas now. You've got to move to Denver, and you're going to make thirty thousand a year more." He doesn't pray. He doesn't ask God, "God, do You want me to do that?" He just says, "Well, it's a no-brainer. Thirty thousand dollars a year more. We're going!"

Why do I ask? It took just as much of the blood of Jesus to save that businessman as it did that preacher. No man, whether he's in the ministry or out of the ministry, has a right to say, "I'm going to make all the money I can, and that's it!" Everybody has to pray and say, "Lord, what is Your will?" I'm not saying it's not God's will for you to make more money. I'm not saying that it's not God's will for a preacher to leave one church to go to another and get a raise, if that's God's plan for him. But, friend, we have to be motivated by one thing, and that is the glory of Jesus Christ. We seek first the kingdom of God and His righteousness, and all these things shall be added unto us.

Give God the First Devotion of Your Heart

Jesus told the church at Ephesus in Revelation 2:4: *"I have somewhat against thee, for thou hast left thy first love."* Not that they didn't love Him anymore; they just didn't love Him with that first love, the honeymoon love.

If you are married, has the honeymoon ever ended in your life? If you don't love your mate more now than you did when you got married, you love him or her less. Love is not static. I am madly in love with my wife of over fifty years. I've got a crush on her, I really do, and the honeymoon has never gone out of our marriage. I love her more than I did when I married her, and I loved her when I married her.

Some of us loved the Lord when we got saved, but the honeymoon is over. Somebody said, "The honeymoon is that period of time between "I do" and "You'd better!" Is your love for Jesus fresh, vibrant, real?

Joyce knows that she's not first place in my heart. She knows that! She knows that she is second place. She knows that Jesus Christ is first place in my life. I know that I'm not first place in Joyce's life. I know I'm second. I don't mind that at all. She doesn't mind at all being second place in my life, because she knows I can love her so much more by putting Jesus Christ first than I could ever love her by putting her first. You see, *"The love of God is shed abroad in our hearts by the Holy Ghost"* (Rom. 5:5). And when Jesus Christ taught us to pray, He included this admonition: *"Seek ye first the kingdom of God and his righteousness . . ."*

The Promise of God's Preeminence

There is a promise that is in this verse, Matthew 6:33: *"Seek ye first the kingdom of God and his righteousness; and all these things shall be added unto you."* Modern Americans try to put things first and God second, and God will not work in second place. Someone has said that we ought to worship God, love people, and use things. But most Americans want to use people, love things, and put God in last place, and that will not work! When he talked about seeking first the kingdom of God and His righteousness, He told us why we worry.

He says in Matthew 6:30–34: *"Wherefore, if God so clothe the grass of the field, which today is, and tomorrow is cast into the oven, shall he not much more clothe you, O ye of little faith? Therefore take no thought, saying, What shall we eat, or what shall we drink? what shall we eat or what shall we drink, or wherewithal shall we be clothed? (For after all these things do the Gentiles seek:) for your heavenly Father knoweth that you have need of all these things. But seek ye first the kingdom of God and his righteousness; and all these things shall be added unto you. Take therefore no thought for the morrow; the morrow shall take thought for the things of itself. Sufficient unto the day is the evil thereof."*

Would you like to know how to cure worry? All you need to do is practice the power of proper priorities. Let me give you a definition of worry. It is putting things first. It is failing to seek first the kingdom of God and His righteousness. What did the master teacher, the Lord Jesus, say about worry?

Worry Is Needless

He said, first of all, it's needless. Matthew 6:25: *"Therefore I say unto you, Take no thought for your life, what ye shall eat, or what ye shall drink; nor yet for your body, what ye shall put on. Is not the life more than meat, and the body more than raiment?"* We have the assurance that He's going to take care of us. Worry is needless. Don't be like the little lady who said, "Don't tell me worry doesn't do any good. Most of the things I worry about never happen!"

Worry Is Senseless

Not only is it needless, it's senseless. Notice the logic of Jesus in Matthew 6:26: *"For behold the fowls of the air; for they sow not, neither do they reap, nor gather into barns: yet your heavenly Father feedeth them. Are ye not much better than they?"* Jesus is saying, "If your Father takes care of the birds, He is certainly going to take care of you. You're His child!" Worry is needless. Therefore, it's senseless.

Worry Is Useless

And worry is useless. Jesus continues in verse 27: *"Which of you by taking thought can add one cubit unto his stature?"* Worry never does any good. It never solves a problem. It never dries a tear. It's not only senseless, it is absolutely useless. It never lifts a burden. There are only two things you should never worry about: those things you can do something about and those things you can't do anything about. If you can do something about it, stop worrying and do it. If you can't do anything about it, worry is not going to change it.

> *For every burden under the sun,*
> *either there's a cure or there is none.*
> *If there be one, seek till ye find it;*
> *if there be none, never mind it.*

Worry Is Faithless

And, friend, worry is faithless. Jesus said, *"If God so clothe the grass of the field, which . . . to morrow is cast into the oven, shall he not much more clothe you, O ye of little faith?"* (Matt. 6:30). Worry says, "God, You're not able to take care of this problem. This problem is too big for You. I'm putting things first."

Worry Is Excuseless

There's no excuse for worry.

I heard about a man named Bob who was failing in life—one of those guys for whom nothing ever seemed to go right. The poor guy tried to be a salesman. He couldn't sell anything. He drove a rusty, shabby old car. Dressed poorly. His wife was homely. His children were failing in school. He lived on the wrong side of the tracks. He was just a dismal failure.

And then one day Bob changed. He began to stand up straight, put a smile on his face, began to whistle, started driving a brand new, shiny automobile, moved into a fine house. His wife fixed herself up. She was actually attractive. His kids began to make passing grades. This guy had a radical transformation.

His friend Jack said, "Bob, I've never seen such a transformation in anybody as I've seen in you. What is your secret?"

Bob said, "Well, first of all, let me tell you what my problem was. It was worry. I realized that. And I knew I needed to do something about it, so I hired a firm of professional worriers."

Jack asked, "How exactly does it work?" Bob said, "Well, rather than worry, you go to that place and you tell them all of your problems, and then you go out and do your job, and they stay there and worry for you, and you don't have to do it."

"Well, I have to admit there's a great transformation," Jack said. "How much does it cost?" Bob replied, "A thousand dollars a week." "Good night! How are you going to pay that?" "Oh," Bob said, "that's their worry!"

Wouldn't it be wonderful if there was someone who could carry the burden for you so you don't have to carry it? Come up close. I want to tell you something. There is! His name is Jesus! And it doesn't cost you a thousand dollars a week. *"Casting all your care upon him, for he careth for you"* (1 Pet. 5:7). *"Seek ye first the kingdom of God, and his righteousness; and all these things shall be added unto you"* (Matt. 6:33).

CHAPTER 3

Our Daily Bread

"The Provision of the Prayer"

"Give us this day our daily bread."
—MATTHEW 6:11

What I want to think about with you in this chapter is praying for daily bread. We could expand this to say, "praying for daily needs." When the Bible says, *"Give us this day our daily bread,"* what Jesus is talking about is not only bread. This is a model prayer. If you need bread, ask for it. Whatever you need, ask God for it, whether it is material, whether it is physical, or whether it is spiritual. If you have a need, you can ask God. But here's how you do it. There are three things you need to consider when praying for daily bread.

Establish a Proper Priority

Before you can ask for daily bread, you must make sure your priorities are correct. As we talked about in the previous chapter, you must start by putting God first: *"Thy name . . . thy kingdom . . . thy will." "Seek first the kingdom of God and His righteousness, and all these things shall be added unto you"* (Matt. 6:30 NKJV).

Have you ever asked for daily bread, but not received it? Are you seeking God first? Prayer is not for the ungodly, and prayer is not for the rebellious. If your life is not surrendered to Him, if you're not putting Him first, if you're not honoring Him, don't be surprised if your prayer is not answered.

I challenge anyone to honestly assert, "I have sought first the kingdom of God and His righteousness, and I've gone lacking in needing things." No one would dare say that because it's not true. God guarantees you, *"Seek first the kingdom of God and His righteousness, and all these things shall be added unto you."*

There was an old saint that used to put T & P in the margin of her Bible. And she had T & P by Matthew 6:33. Somebody asked her, "What does that T & P mean?" She said, "It means tried and proven." Tried and proven. *"Seek first the kingdom of God and His righteousness, and all these things shall be added unto you."*

Think about it. *"Give us this day our daily bread."* What is bread for? Bread is to nourish you, to give you strength to do what you ought to do. Question: Why should God give you strength to serve the devil or to fulfill your own selfish desires?

When I was in college, I worked at the A&P grocery store to help pay my tuition. I remember one time when I was walking home from work, I was hungry and I stopped to eat at a diner. I reached my hand in my pocket. I had twenty-one cents. That's all I had in this whole wide world, just twenty-one cents.

I looked at the menu and there was a cheese sandwich for twenty cents. That was the only thing on the menu for twenty cents. The lady behind the counter said, "What do you want?" I said, "I'd like a cheese sandwich, please." She said, "Do you want anything to drink?" I said, "A glass of water, please." I walked out of there without an empty pocket. I still had a penny in my pocket. I can tell you this: I can say with David, *"I have been young, and now I'm old; yet have I not seen the righteous forsaken, nor his seed begging bread"* (Ps. 37:25).

Another time, I was working a construction job for McLaren Construction Company. We were remodeling a building called the Mercantile Building in West Palm Beach, Florida. We were pouring a cement floor. At 4:30, the normal time to stop work, we couldn't stop work, because the cement was wet and the job was not finished. We had to keep on wheeling those wheelbarrows in, and dumping the cement over that rebar, and letting the finishers come by and finish the work.

While we were working, I looked up and Mr. McLaren had shown up with some of the finest sandwiches I'd ever seen—big, fat meaty sandwiches, and wheelbarrows full of soft drinks. He said, "Men, just keep working, but help yourself. Just don't stop. Just keep working, but work and eat, stop and eat a little bit, but just keep working." I thought about that later on. *Why did Mr. McLaren do all of that? Why did he go out and buy those sandwiches and soft drinks for us?* I'll tell you why. We were working for him. He wanted us to be strong. He didn't want us to stop. I don't think Mr. McLaren would have bought us those sandwiches if we had not been working for him. And especially if we had been working for the competition.

Why does God give us daily bread? God gives us bread so we can serve Him. Bread is for strength. Strength is for service. If you're not living for God, don't expect Him to feed you. Don't expect Him to answer your prayers to give you more strength to serve the devil. You must establish a proper priority. Do you want your prayers answered? Do you want daily bread? You must first establish a proper priority.

Express a Practical Petition

Sometimes people think that you can't ask God for things. You certainly can ask God for things. If you need things, you ask God. God answers practical, personal petitions. Don't think that you can only pray and ask God to make you a better soul winner, or help you to understand the Bible better. Now He will do that. But if you need bread, ask God for bread. Matthew 7:11: *"If ye then, being evil, know how to give good gifts unto your children, how much more shall your Father which is in heaven give good things to them that ask him?"* James 4:2 says, *"Ye have not, because ye ask not."*

Did you know that God delights to give things to His children? But James says that often we have not because we ask not. The great mystery in the world today is not unanswered prayer; it is unoffered prayer. Why don't we pray?

When I was in college, I pastored a little church in Fellsmere, Florida, a little sugar mill town on the edge of the Everglades. There was a deacon in that church named Mr. Ingram, who had some wonderful citrus trees on his property. It was in the Indian River section of Florida, between Fort Pierce and Vero Beach where they grow some of the best oranges and grapefruit in the world.

One day, Mr. Ingram said to me, "Adrian, I want to give you some oranges," and he gave me a duffel bag full of fruit. I said, "Mr. Ingram, I can't eat all that fruit." "Well," he said, "take it back with you, and give it to some of the other students there at college." When I got back to the college apartment where Joyce and I lived, I lugged that great big heavy bagful of oranges up those two flights of stairs, and put them in a closet. So I had a closet full of oranges.

The next day, Joyce and I were having lunch, and we were sitting by the window. And I was looking down into the back yard of our little apartment where there was a sour orange tree. A sour orange is an ornamental shrub. The oranges are beautiful, but, friend, they're not fit for man or beast to eat. One bite of a sour orange and you would have lockjaw.

As I was looking down there, and I saw a little boy walking around in our backyard. And I said, "What is that kid doing down there?" He was looking very suspicious, this way and that way, but he failed to look up. That's what most of us do. We're trying to keep others from finding out what we're up to, and God sees it all. In a minute, it dawned on me he was going to steal an orange, one of those sour oranges.

I watched him as he got a hold of a leaf and then got hold of a twig and got the limb down and finally unhooked that orange, put it under his arm, looked around again to make sure no one saw him, and he took off. Now I didn't have any extra money in those days, but I believe I would have given a dollar to see him take the first bite.

Later, I thought about that kid swiping that sour orange. Had he come and knocked on my door and said, "Mister, can I have one of those oranges?" I would have said, "Absolutely not. But, son, if you want oranges, come up here. I'll load you down with oranges." Friend, I had a closet full of oranges. I had oranges that were beginning to spoil. I had oranges I needed to unload and get rid of. If he'd only asked, he could have had some of the best oranges in the whole wide world. But he didn't ask.

I believe one of these days, when I get to heaven, God may say, "Adrian, let's take a walk." And He's going to come to a particular place, and He's going to open a door and say, "Adrian, look in there." I'll say, "Lord, what are all those wonderful things?" "Those were things I wanted to give you, but you didn't ask." *"You have not because you ask not."* I wonder how many blessings there are in heaven that you and I have failed to apprehend, failed to appropriate, failed to receive because we've failed to ask. God wants to answer our prayer. He says, *"Call unto me, and I will answer thee, and show thee great and mighty things which thou knowest not"* (Jer. 33:3). *"Ask, and ye shall receive,"* the Bible teaches, *"that your joy may be full."* So ask God if you need something.

Your Need, Not Your Greed

That doesn't mean you can have everything you want. The Bible says in Philippians 4:19: *"My God shall supply all your need according to His riches in glory in Christ Jesus"* (NKJV). God promises to supply our need, not our greed.

Sometimes we want things we don't need. Sometimes we need things we don't want. My dad used to say, "You need a spanking." He was right. I didn't want one, but I did need one. But whatever we need, we can come to God and ask if the giving of it will make us more like Jesus in the receiving of it. And no detail is too small to be an object of prayer. If it concerns you, it concerns God. Don't say, "Well, it's too small to pray about." Can you think of anything that's big to God? The biggest thing you've got is still small to God. And God wants to answer your prayer.

One of my favorite Scriptures is Romans 8:32. It says, *"He that spared not his own son, but delivered him up for us all, how shall he not with him also freely give us all things?"*

Think about Paul's logic in this verse: *"He that spared not his own son, but delivered him up freely for us all . . ."* Do you know if there were ever a promise that God would have been tempted to go back on, it would have been the promise to send Jesus? If He kept that promise, you can count on Him keeping any other promise.

Suppose you were to come to me and say, "Adrian, can I have one of your sons?" "What do you want to do with my son?" "Well, I want to sacrifice him." "Why do you want to sacrifice him?" "I want to sacrifice your son for somebody else's wickedness, for somebody else's sin. But I want to torture him first and then sacrifice him. Will you give me your son?" I'd say, "No, no. You can't have my son. I wouldn't give you my son. I would not deliver my son up to you to be tortured, butchered, massacred for somebody else's sin." But suppose you could persuade me to give you my son to die, to be butchered on a cross. And then you said, "Now, since you have given me your son, will you also give me his bicycle and his basketball?" Friend, that would be a no-brainer. If I gave you my son, I wouldn't have to worry about giving you his bicycle or basketball or anything else. If I loved you enough to give my son, would I not give anything else? You think about the logic. *". . . how shall he not also with him freely give us all things."* We can ask God for what we need. And we don't have to have anything else except His grace and our faith.

I've seen God do things that are just incredible in prayer. And I certainly don't hold myself up as a paragon of excellence in prayer, but I believe in prayer, and I pray faithfully, and God answers my prayers. If He doesn't give me what I ask, He gives me something better than I asked.

When we lived in Florida, one time I took Joyce out to lunch. And when we came home from lunch, I just kind of brushed my hip where I keep my billfold, and there was no billfold there. I said, "Joyce, have you seen my billfold?" "No." We looked around the house. It wasn't there. I said, "I wonder if I left it in the restaurant." Went back to the restaurant. It wasn't there.

I had credit cards in the billfold. I had a voter registration card. I had a driver's license in there. I had an old Roman coin that somebody had given me. And I had about three or four dollars. I didn't mind the three or four dollars, but I hated to lose the old Roman coin, and I certainly hated to lose the credit cards and the driver's license. I got perturbed thinking about all the aggravation about having to replace everything.

I was going back to my office and I fell under great conviction. I said, "God, I am so sorry. I've been more concerned about a lost billfold than I have lost souls. Forgive me. I have misplaced priorities. Why am I so upset about something like that more than souls that don't know the Lord Jesus Christ? God, have mercy on me. I will not worry about it. I turn that over to You. Thank You, Lord."

Now, here's the strange thing. That night, just before I went to bed, I prayed a prayer. I said, "Lord, would You show me in a dream where my billfold is?" Friend, that was strange for me to pray that. I've never prayed and asked God to show me anything in a dream before that or after that.

I went to sleep and I had a dream. I dreamed about my billfold, and I saw it. It was in one of these big blue mailboxes that says US Mail on the side. I had x-ray vision in my dream. I could see right through that mailbox, and could see my billfold inside. And I could see right through the billfold. I saw all my credit cards. I saw the driver's license. I saw the Roman coin. And I saw there was no money in there.

"If God doesn't give me what I ask, He gives me something better than I asked."

Next morning, when I woke up, I went to my office. When I walked in, my secretary said, "The postmaster is on the phone, and wants to talk to you." I said, "Fine, put him on." I said, "Before you tell me," I said, "I'm going to tell you. You have my billfold, don't you?" He said, "I sure do." I said, "Now don't tell me where it was. Let me tell you. It was in one of those big blue mailboxes, wasn't it?" He said, "It sure was." I said, "Now let me tell you there's no money in it, but there's an old Roman coin and all my papers, and so forth in there." He said, "Mister, how do you know all that?" I guess he thought maybe I'd dropped it in there. I've thought about that. Friend, there is no way on this earth that could have happened apart from God revealing to me and answering my prayer, telling me exactly, specifically what I asked Him to do.

But I thought, *Now, why? What purpose did it serve?* I would have gotten the billfold anyway. I committed it to the Lord. The Lord knew where it was. I really believe the Lord was just showing me, "Adrian, you were right to say you're not going to worry about it. I knew where it was, and I could show you if I needed to show where it was. Just trust Me, Adrian."

Exercise a Personal Plan

Prayer is no substitute for diligence. It is no substitute for obedience. It is no substitute for work. And, as a matter of fact, the Bible says, "Faith without works is dead." If a man wants a house and prays for a house, he can say amen with a hammer and saw. If he prays for a girlfriend, he ought to learn good manners and he ought to learn how to pursue her.

People say, "You know, God feeds the birds." Well, God does feed the birds, but they have to scratch for it. The house we used to live in had a lot of leaves on the ground. And in the spring when the robins would come, I used to marvel at the robins out there turning over leaves looking for worms. They work for it; God doesn't throw it in the nest.

If you ask God for bread, God will give you bread. However, in Genesis 3:19, God says: *"In the sweat of thy face shalt thou eat bread."* In Second Thessalonians 3:10, Paul says, *"For even when we were with you, this we commanded you that if any would not work, neither should he eat."* Paul said a man who refuses to work should not expect to eat. Proverbs 20:4: *"The sluggard will not plow by reason of the cold; therefore shall he beg in harvest and have nothing."* Proverbs 28:19: *"He that tilleth his land shall have plenty of bread."*

So prayer is not a substitute for work. It's not a substitute for diligence. Even if you have plenty of bread, you still ought to work. Why? So you can give bread to other people who have need. The Bible says we're to support those who have need. Here's what Paul said in Acts 20:35, *"I have shown you in every way, by laboring like this, that you must support the weak. And remember the words of the Lord Jesus, that He said, 'It is more blessed to give than to receive'"* (NKJV).

Suppose God blesses you financially to the point that you have more than you will ever need to eat. Does that mean you stop working? No. Retirement, fine; indolence, no. Pray for daily bread. When you have plenty, keep on being productive. Then you've got more and more to give away.

Enjoy a Present Provision

You don't need a lot of bread. All you need is enough bread. The Bible says that if you have food and clothes, you should be content. To whom little is not enough, nothing is enough. You don't need a warehouse full of bread. You need daily bread. Let me ask you a question. Which had you rather have—a warehouse full of stale bread or a father that owns a bakery?

I had a boy tell me one time, "God has called me to preach, but I can't go to school." I said, "Well, why not?" He said, "I don't have the money to go." I said, "God has called you?" "Oh, yes, God has called me." "But you can't go?" "No!" "Why?" "I don't have the money." I said, "If I could get a millionaire to underwrite your expenses, would you go?" "Wow," he said, "I sure would." I said, "Well, friend, you've got the one that owns the world, Almighty God."

Don't you know that if God called this boy to go to school that God, in some way, is going to meet his need? Of course, He will. God gives us our daily bread. *"My God shall supply all your need according to His riches in glory by Christ Jesus"* (Phil. 4:19).

Now if you've got bread for today, thank Him. And, as Jesus said, *"Take therefore no thought for the morrow: the morrow shall take thought for the things of itself"* (Matt. 6:34). The Bible is not against planning. The Bible says that the ant provides her meat in the summertime for the winter, and all of that. I know that. But when you worry about it, you're not trusting God. You're putting things first, rather than God first. *"Seek first the kingdom of God and His righteousness, and all these things will be added to you"* (Matt. 6:33 NKJV).

Many of us would say that we believe that, but our actions don't back it up. Friend, I didn't say that. Jesus said it! *"Seek first the kingdom of God and His righteousness, and all these things shall be added to you."* Now most of us say, "Yes, but I've got to have something to fall back on." Fall back on God. Fall back on Jesus.

Years ago, I went to hear an evangelist speak. He said something and I'll never forget it. He said, "I don't need any money." Well, when you're living on love offerings, that's not the thing you usually say. He said, "I don't need any money." And I sat up straight and listened. I'd always heard preachers say, "I need money." I've heard people who go out there and twist arms to get people to give. He said, "I don't need any money." I thought, *I wonder what his source is.* And then here's what he said. "My wife and I have forty dollars in the bank." He said, "We don't need any money until that's gone." I learned a lesson from that evangelist. I don't know what he preached. I couldn't tell you his text. I couldn't tell you anything else, but that has stuck with me. Friend, we enjoy a present provision, day by day trusting the Lord.

Keep Your Arms Up

Have you ever seen a trolley car that has an arm that goes up and runs with electric current? It just runs along, but everywhere it goes, the arm reaches up there hooked to that wire. Most of us drive automobiles that have a gas tank. When we get low on gas, we have to go fill it up or the car stops running. But the trolley just keeps its arm up. It hooks onto that wire. And as long as it stays in contact with that wire, it has all it needs to keep on running.

Most of us want to operate like the automobile. We want enough gas in the car to take us where we feel we need to go. Well, that's one way to live. But another way to live is just to stay in contact with the heavenly Father. Abide in Him. *"But my God shall supply all your need, according to his riches in glory by Christ Jesus"* (Phil. 4:19).

CHAPTER 4

The Freedom of Forgiveness

"The Pardon of the Prayer"

"And forgive us our debts, as we forgive our debtors."
—Matthew 6:12

Think with me about the freedom of forgiveness. When you are forgiven, you are set free. When you forgive another person, you set them free. And when you forgive another person, not only do you set them free, but you set yourself free. So we're going to talk about how to live free.

There are two great problems that come to the human psyche: one is guilt and the other is bitterness. We have guilt because of what we have done. You ask the average person, "What is guilt?" and he'll say, "Oh, that's the feeling you have when you do something wrong." No, that's not guilt. That is the guilt feeling. If you put your hand on a hot stove and it gets burned and there's a blister there, I would ask you, "What is the burn?" You would say, "That is the feeling you feel when you put your hand on a hot stove." No. The blister is the burn; the feeling is the result of the blister. The guilt feeling is the result of the guilt. The worst thing in the world that you could ever do would be to try to kill the feeling without dealing with the guilt. Guilt is one of the wounds that come to the human psyche. It will not heal until it is dealt with. It will fester until it is cleansed. And guilt comes to us by something we have done wrong.

There's another wound that comes to the human psyche, and that is bitterness. Bitterness is resentment because of what someone else has done to you—real or perceived. They may not really have done you wrong, but you perceive that they have. And, nonetheless, perception may be the cruelest form of reality. But you feel somebody has done you wrong. Guilt and bitterness both have to be dealt with by forgiveness. And our Lord, knowing the deep needs that we have, taught us to pray, "And forgive us our debts, as we forgive our debtors." Why did He say, "our debts"? Because sin is a debt.

We have sinned against heaven. We're guilty of high treason against heaven's King. We have used God's resources illegally because we were not giving Him the praise, the glory, the worship that is due to His name. In a sense, we have robbed Him. We have defrauded Him. And we have been sued by heaven for damages. Now when God forgives, He cancels the debt. Forgiveness is the canceling of a debt.

If you owed me a thousand dollars, and you came to me and said, "Adrian, I owe you this thousand dollars, but I cannot pay you. Would you please forgive the debt?" Suppose I did forgive it. Then, what has it cost me? A thousand dollars.

There are no bargain pardons. To forgive is costly. It costs to forgive. When God forgives us, does He say, "Oh, well, that's all right; don't worry about it. It wasn't that bad; I'm a loving God." Oh, no. Ephesians 1:7 says, *"In whom we have redemption through his blood, the forgiveness of sins."* For me to be forgiven by our Lord cost the rich, red, royal blood of the Son of God— the silver of His tears, and the gold of His blood. You see, forgiveness costs. When you forgive someone, it is costly. That's the reason we say that grace is G-R-A-C-E—God's Riches at Christ's Expense.

What a joy to experience the freedom of forgiveness—learning to set others free. When we're forgiven, God sets us free. When we forgive someone else, we set them free. But, at the same time, we, again, are setting ourselves free.

The Compelling Reasons for Forgiveness

Here are some reasons why you need to learn to forgive:

The Grace Factor

We have received grace; therefore, we need to give it. Ephesians 4:32 is a great verse. You may know it. You might have it on the refrigerator; or perhaps have taught it to your children: *"Be ye kind, tenderhearted, forgiving one another, even as God for Christ's sake hath forgiven you."* If you have received grace, then you need to give grace. God has been so good to me. Therefore, I need to be good to you.

I read one time of a man who was an employee who embezzled several hundred dollars. When the books were checked, this man was discovered. He was called up to the chief executive's office. He trudged up the stairs afraid. He knew what was going to happen. He knew what he deserved. He expected to be, at the best, dismissed; at the worst, brought into court and perhaps go to jail.

He went and stood in front of that big desk. The executive looked up and said, "Is it true that you have done this thing you have been accused of?" The employee knew that it did not make sense to deny it. He bowed his head. He said, "Yes, sir, it is true. I am guilty." He wasn't expecting what was to come next. The executive said to him, "I want to ask you a question. If I were to forgive and keep you in your present responsibility, from this point forward, could I trust you?" The man said, "Sir, if you would give me a second chance, I promise you from the depth of my heart, and with all of my being, you can trust me." The man said, "Very well. You will not be charged and you will not be dismissed. But I want you to know something. You are not the first man to have received mercy in this business. I was the first one. I did something exactly as you did, and I was forgiven and reinstated. The mercy that I have received I'm extending to you. And may God have mercy upon us both."

You see, you have received grace. I have received grace. And because we have received grace, we need to give grace. An old Methodist evangelist, Sam Jones, said, "I made up my mind that I would never fall out with anybody until he treated me worse than I treated Jesus." Friend, if God has forgiven us, then we need to be kind, tenderhearted, forgiving one another, as God for Christ's sake hath forgiven us.

A lady wrote me a letter a while back. She said, "I'm from Rome, Georgia. I was over in Memphis and I needed emergency surgery. I didn't have friends over here. I needed blood. Two young men from your church came over and donated blood for me." She said, "They did not even leave their name. I don't know who they are, but they left a note and here's what the note said: 'We gave our blood for you because Jesus gave His for us.'" Think about that. 'We gave our blood for you because Jesus gave His for us.' That lady said, "Pastor, I don't know who your young men are, but if you can find any way to thank them, I want you to thank them." Friend, if Jesus gave His blood for us, the least we can do is to give forgiveness and grace to one another.

The Guilt Factor

There is another reason that we need to forgive, and that is the guilt factor. You and I need to be forgiven. Jesus said if we refuse to forgive others, we ourselves cannot be forgiven. In Matthew 6:14–15, Jesus said, *"For if ye forgive men their trespasses, your heavenly Father will also forgive you: But if ye forgive not men their trespasses, neither will your Father forgive your trespasses."*

Here is something to think about: Unforgiveness is ungodly because God is a God of forgiveness. And if you're not a forgiving person, you are ungodly. It's not just that you have failed to do something nice if you don't forgive. You are ungodly. And unforgiveness, as long as it remains unforgiveness, is unforgivable. The person who will not forgive another person destroys the bridge over which he himself needs to travel. Only the person who never does anything wrong, only the person who never sins, is the person who can refuse to forgive other people and still be right with God.

In the model prayer, our Lord taught us to pray, *"And forgive us our debts, as we forgive our debtors"* (Matt. 6:12). Or the Tyndale translation: *"Forgive us our trespasses, as we forgive those who trespass against us."* That's a dangerous prayer if you don't want to forgive other people. What you're saying is, "Lord, You treat me like I treat others." Would you like God to treat you like you treat others? What if you said, "He did me wrong. I'm never going to have anything else to do with him." Do you want God to say, "You did Me wrong. I'll never have anything else to do with you"? What if you said to someone who hurt you, "I'll forgive, but I won't forget." Do you want God to say, "I'll forgive you, but I won't forget"? No, friend. That is a dangerous prayer if you don't mean to forgive others.

Jesus told an interesting story about a man who owed an enormous debt (see Matt. 18:23–35). The debt was equal to billions of dollars. He couldn't pay, and the king knew he couldn't pay, but the king forgave him anyway. Then this same man went out and found someone else who owed him a hundred denari, a hundred days' wages.

> *"Unforgiveness is unforgivable."*

He took this other man by the scruff of the neck and said, "If you don't pay me what you owe me, I'm going to cast you into prison." When the king heard what the first man had done who had been forgiven, he was angry. As the King James says, *"He was wroth!"* He was steamed, he was hacked, he was angry, and rightly so. The king then took that man who had been forgiven, rescinded it all, cast him into prison. What's our Lord saying? He's saying, "How dare we have the unmitigated gall to refuse to forgive someone else when God has forgiven us so much."

The Grief Factor

Here's another reason to forgive—the grief factor. If we don't forgive someone else, we ourselves are the one who is going to suffer grief. If you say, "I am going to make them suffer," friend, you will suffer also. If you say, "I'm not going to let them off the hook," then *you* are on the hook.

In Hebrews 12:15, God says that we're to be *"looking diligently lest any man fail of the grace of God; lest any root of bitterness springing up trouble you, and thereby many be defiled."*

A root is that which is underground. If you're like many people in this world, you might have underground bitterness. It doesn't show on your face right now. But down beneath the surface is a nauseous root. And some day it will spring up. And when it springs up, it will trouble you. And not only will it trouble you, many are going to be defiled. Bitterness is a terrible thing, and the grief it causes is horrible.

Paul says in Ephesians 4:31: *"Let all bitterness, and wrath, and anger, and clamor, and evil speaking, be put away from you, with all malice."* Let's start at the beginning of this verse: *"Let all bitterness . . ."* What is bitterness? Bitterness is the result of a wound that has come to you. As I've said before, it may be real, it may be perceived, but, nonetheless, you have taken it in. Somebody has hurt you. And you mull it over. You don't deal with it. It becomes a root. It may be underground—a root of bitterness. Paul continues, *"Let all bitterness, and wrath . . ."*

What is the word *wrath*? It comes from a Greek word that means, "to get hot, to burn." You do sort of a slow burn. It's like oily rags in a closet. Somehow, they begin to generate heat. They just sit there and smolder. That's wrath. It's the slow burn. It comes from bitterness. Now watch this. *"Let all bitterness, and wrath, and anger . . ."*

What is anger? Anger is the outward expression of that bitterness and wrath. Somebody opens the door. You never know when it's going to happen. And the air hits those oily rags and they burst into flame. Have you ever seen people just, seemingly, fly off the handle and get just angry, all of a sudden? You say, "What happened?" Well, it started a long time ago with bitterness. That was the slow burn, and now it becomes the open flame of anger.

But the devil is not finished yet. The bitterness turns to wrath, and the wrath turns to anger, and the anger turns to clamor. What is clamor? It is loud speaking. Have you ever noticed that when people get in arguments, they raise their voice? And one person will say to the other one, "Stop shouting." The other will shout back, "I'm not shouting!" Voices are raised in clamor, blood pressure rises, temper intensifies, and the devil says to himself, "You two are doing great. Keep it up!"

Next, clamor turns to evil speaking. Have you ever noticed that when people get angry, they say some terrible things? "I wish you'd never been born." "I wish we had never been married." "I hate you." "You're so stupid." They begin to say terrible, horrible things—things they don't really mean. But somehow they're on a roll. They started with bitterness, then wrath, then anger, then clamor, then evil speaking. And finally, evil speaking ends in malice.

Malice means that you want to hurt somebody. You want to do them harm. There's a man who loves his darling wife, but he gets in an argument, and that bitterness—he's never forgiven her for something—becomes anger, and then clamor, then evil speaking, and finally, malice. He shoves her; she reaches up and throws something; one of them slaps the other in the face, or worse.

And they wish a thousand worlds that they'd never done it, but they did it. Where does it start? With bitterness. Bitterness that they let get down in their heart. And they will not let it go! Why do we forgive? *The grace factor*—we've been forgiven. *The guilt factor*—we need to be forgiven. *The grief factor*—if we don't, we will suffer grief, they will suffer grief, others will suffer grief.

You say, "Well, I'm not going to let them off the hook." You're on the hook with them. You say, "Well, I'm going to get even." Do you really want to get even? If they've harmed you, you're up here and they're down here. When you get even, what do you do? That's just what you do—you get even. You put yourself down on their level. Why not just forgive?

The Gain Factor

Let me tell you another reason that we need to forgive: it's *the gain factor.* When we forgive, we gain a brother. Jesus said that if you go to church and you're getting ready to make your offering and you remember that your brother has something against you, leave your offering there and go and make it right with your brother, and then come and make your offering (see Matt. 5:24).

If you're trying to worship God with bitterness in your heart, forget it. If you've wronged somebody and haven't made it right, or there's somebody that you won't forgive, leave the gift. You can't buy God off. I don't care how much you give. Don't take that money and spend it because it's "tainted money." 'Tain't yours. But leave it and go be reconciled and then come and worship. Again, Matthew 18:15: *"If thy brother shall trespass against thee, go and tell him his fault between thee and him alone: if he shall hear thee, thou hast gained thy brother."* The first verse said be reconciled to your brother. That verse says you have gained your brother. A brother is a precious thing. Why lose a brother? Why lose a sister? Why not be reconciled? Have you ever seen brothers and sisters who grew up together get in an argument over a family inheritance or something? And they lose a brother, they lose a sister, good friends sometimes, over some foolish, silly thing.

Years ago, one of my dear friends did me wrong. It wasn't a big thing, but I felt it was an act of dishonesty, and a little bit of a betrayal. And my first thought was, *Well, I don't need him. I can get along without him. I've got other people that I can associate with.* Then I thought, *Adrian, you're a fool, you're a fool. That man is a good friend, and you need to forgive*, which I did, and today he's one of my very best friends.

Why should I lose the fellowship and the fun and the friendship that I have with that brother when we can be reconciled?

I heard a story about a man who got marooned on a desert island. After he had been there for what seemed like an eternity, he was finally found. His rescuers noticed there were three huts on that island. They asked him, "Who is here with you?" He said, "No one, just me." "Then why do you have three huts?" He said, "Well, the first one is where I live. The other two are churches." They asked, "But why two churches? You're here by yourself." "Oh," he said, "I got mad at the first one and moved my membership." Isn't it sad that people in churches can't get along? Churches are split over these things. When people can't get along, there are four results:

- It disgraces the Father.
- It discourages the saints.
- It drives away the lost.
- It delights the devil.

The Bible says, *"How good and how pleasant it is for brethren to dwell together in unity!"* (Ps. 133:1).

The Costly Requirements of Forgiveness

Remember I told you that to forgive is costly? Jesus is the model. *"Be ye kind, tenderhearted, forgiving one another, even as God for Christ's sake hath forgiven you."* What are the requirements for forgiveness?

Forgive Freely

First of all, forgive freely. Does God forgive us freely? Absolutely! Do you have to beg God for forgiveness? No. God is knocking at your heart's door wanting to forgive you. God chases us to forgive us.

When Adam and Eve sinned in the Garden of Eden, did God say, "Well, I'm going to sit up here in heaven and let them see if they can find me?" No. God came down to the garden, and God cried out, "Adam, where are you?" That wasn't the voice of a detective. That was the voice of a brokenhearted God who was seeking him out to forgive. When they were nailing Jesus to the cross, Jesus was praying, "Father, forgive them, for they know not what they do."

Jesus said in Matthew 18, "If your brother sins against you, go to your brother alone. Tell him his fault between the two of you. And if he will hear you, you have gained your brother." Peter, in Matthew 18:21, asked this question: *"Lord, how oft shall my brother sin against me and I forgive him? Till seven times?"* You know, seven is the perfect number. Peter thought, *I've really done a lot if I forgive my brother seven times. "And Jesus saith unto him, I say not unto thee until seven times, but until seventy times seven"* (v. 22). He didn't mean 490; He meant as many times as he needs to be forgiven. What Jesus was saying is: Forget the math. Keeping count has nothing to do with it. Just keep forgiving. And love does not keep account of that forgiveness. We are to forgive freely. If there's somebody who's done you wrong, don't wait for them to come to you; go to them.

Forgive Fully

Not only forgive freely, but forgive fully. Now don't pretend that it doesn't matter. If someone comes to you and says, "Thus and such have I done, would you please forgive me?" If we really want to act big, we'll say, "Don't worry about it. That's okay. Don't worry about it." Friend, when you forgive somebody, don't just say, "Oh, don't worry about it." Say, "I forgive you." And mean it. Forgive fully. Don't just say, "Forget it." You can't forget it until it is forgiven. And if you have wronged somebody and they come to you and tell you about it, don't do what so many do—what our human pride wants us to do. They say, "Oh, look, if I hurt you, I'm sorry; I apologize." Friend, saying, "If

I have hurt you" won't cut it. If you've hurt them, say, "I hurt you." Confess it fully. And then don't say, "I apologize." The word *apologize* comes from a Greek word *apologia*. It gives us the theological term *apologetics*. And what is apologetics? It is a legal defense. It is an argument for what you believe. Don't say, "I apologize." Say, "I was wrong; forgive me." People don't need an apology; they need a confession. And you don't need to say, "Forget it." You need to say, "I forgive." Forgive freely.

Forgive Finally

Forgive finally. That is, when it's buried in the grave of God's forgetfulness, don't keep digging it up again. We're to forgive as God forgives us, *". . . as God for Christ's sake hath forgiven [us]"* (Eph. 4:32). And how does God forgive us? Isaiah 43:25: *"I, even I, am he that blotteth out thy transgressions for mine own sake, and I will not remember thy sins."* Now that brings up an intellectual problem. God is omniscient. Can God ever learn or forget anything? Not in that sense He cannot. But God says, *"I will not remember thy sins."* That is, "I don't remember them now as sins. I remember them as forgiven sins. I will not bring them up again. I will not fling them in your face." And we're to forgive others, *". . . even as God for Christ's sake hath forgiven [us]."*

A businessman saved every piece of correspondence, every bill, every memento. He had them all filed away. His secretary said, "Our files are getting overloaded. We don't have room to put all this stuff. Would you let us clean the files?" After a while, the man reluctantly said, "Okay, okay. You're right. Go ahead. Clean the files. But before you throw anything away, make a copy of it." Isn't that what we do? It is so hard to let it go! But forgive it finally.

Forgive It Forcefully

Forgive it forcefully. What does that mean? Forgiveness is not primarily an emotion. And don't even wait for the emotion. Just simply forgive. You say, "Where do I get the strength to forgive?" To err is human; to forgive is divine. It is God in you, the one who has forgiven you, who will enable you to forgive others. *"Be ye kind, tenderhearted, forgiving one another, even as God for Christ's sake hath forgiven you"* (Eph. 4:32). Where do you get that kindness? Where do you get that tender heart? That's not human nature. That is divine nature, and it takes God for you to do that.

You may have heard of Corrie ten Boom who is now in heaven. But she was a Dutch girl back during World War II who helped to hide the Jews from the Nazis, who were putting them in concentration camps and gas chambers. Finally, they discovered Corrie ten Boom and her sister and family were doing that.

And Corrie and her sister were put in a Nazi concentration camp at Ravensbrook. And she was humiliated in that concentration camp. Her sister died. Corrie survived, but she went through brutality and shame. And there was one particular guard who took great delight in taunting this young Dutch girl. He would do such things as make her strip all of her clothes off and take a shower in front of him while he would stand there and make lewd remarks and taunt her and make vulgar suggestions and humiliate her terribly. But she survived. She came out of that death camp and God used her mightily to share the love of Jesus Christ.

One day, when she was in Europe, she was giving a lecture and she was talking on forgiveness. At the end of that lecture she was shaking hands with the people, and she looked up and saw the face of that very same prison guard, who to her face, his face was a mirror of evil. And he came up with a smile on his hand, and put his hand out to Corrie ten Boom, and said, "Isn't God's forgiveness wonderful?" And he reached his hand out for her to shake hands with him.

Corrie recalled, "I froze. I said, 'God, I cannot shake that man's hand. Jesus, help me.'" And she said, "I felt the love of God flow through my body. And I reached out and took his hand and blessed him in the name of Jesus." Now, friend, that's not human; that's supernatural. That's something only Jesus can do. And to forgive takes the power of God. Forgive forcefully. Mean it with all of your heart.

The Certain Results of Forgiveness

There are no bargain pardons, but forgiveness is still worth it. You know, if you get a bargain sometime, it's really not worth it. The bitterness of poor quality lingers long after the sweetness of cheap price has been forgotten. Although it may be costly, here's what happens when you forgive:

There Will Be Personal Emancipation

First, there will be personal emancipation. When you forgive, you will be set free. Remember the two problems we have—guilt and bitterness? God's forgiveness takes care of our guilt. Our forgiveness takes care of our bitterness along with any continued guilt that we would have, because we can't be forgiven unless we do forgive. But we are set free. We are emancipated. Thank God that we are out of the prison house of guilt and bitterness.

There Will Be Mutual Reconciliation

Second, there will be mutual reconciliation. We're going to find out that it's much more fun to live with friends than it is with enemies; that we're not carrying around that load of bitterness. Now that brings up a real question. "What if the person that has sinned against me just keeps on sinning? I mean, if a person is hitting me on the head and saying, 'Forgive me, forgive me, forgive me,' and keeps bonking me, what do I do about that? What do I do about the person who won't change and is hurting me? Can I forgive them? I mean, after all, God doesn't forgive without repentance. Can I forgive a person who doesn't repent, who's not sorry? How do I handle that?" Let me tell you how to handle it. You offer the forgiveness, even if they can't receive it. You offer it. If you have to, put it in heaven's bank in escrow.

There was a person who hurt someone that I love very deeply and very badly, someone that I love with all my heart. And that person hurt that someone. And I can tell you it hurt me. So much it hurt me. And I thought, *What am I going to do? Can I let this become bitterness? I'm willing to forgive this person, but this person is continuing to do the same thing. How can I forgive?*

> *"God's forgiveness takes care of our guilt; our forgiveness takes care of our bitterness."*

I sat up late at night, about two o'clock in the morning, and I wrote a full letter of forgiveness. Not merely forgiving, but receiving this individual back as a friend and a brother. I wrote it as sincerely as I could, completely, fully, honestly forgiving. I've never delivered that letter because I've not yet had the repentance on that person's part. But, friend, I don't bear the grudge. It's out of my heart. I mean, I have put it in the bank. It's there. All he has to do is write a check of repentance and faith and it's already on escrow. I've already uploaded it. It's gone. It's not on me. I have forgiven, even if he hasn't received it. One day, I hope he will; I hope he will fully. But I am not going to carry around that bitterness in my heart. It is gone; I am free.

So there will be, first of all, that personal emancipation. Then there will be (in most cases) that mutual reconciliation.

There Will Be Spiritual Rejuvenation

And, finally, there will be that spiritual rejuvenation. Do you want revival? Don't just get right with God. Get right with other people. Let me tell you what real revival is. Real revival is not just getting the roof off; it's getting the walls down. Many of us can get the roof off. We say, "You know, God, I want You to forgive me . . ." But we also need to get the walls down and remove that barrier between us and a brother or a sister. When, in a church, not only does the roof get off, but the walls come down, friend, then you have revival.

Perhaps you have heard the name Bertha Smith, one of Southern Baptists' premier missionaries. She said, "The great Shantung Revival began in Shantung, China, when the missionaries who had little petty differences and resentments and bitterness finally confessed their sins one to another. When the missionaries themselves had mutual reconciliation, the great Shantung Revival was on its way.

I want revival. I want it in my own heart. I want it in our churches across the land. *"Our Father, which art in heaven. Hallowed be thy name. Thy kingdom come. Thy will be done on earth, as it is in heaven. Give us this day our daily bread. And forgive our debts, as we forgive our debtors."*

CHAPTER 5

Deliver Us from Evil

"The Protection of the Prayer"

"Lead us not into temptation, but deliver us from evil."
—MATTHEW 6:13

In the Sunday school class, they were going to pray for some missionaries, and the teacher said, "Now the missionaries are very busy. So when you write them and tell them that you are praying for them, don't expect them to write back." One little girl wrote and said, "Dear Missionary, We want you to know we are praying for you. We don't expect an answer."

Are you praying and expecting an answer? I can tell you that if you will get your heart right and pray as Jesus taught you to pray, you will get an answer. And that brings us now to verse 13. *"And lead us not into temptation, but deliver us from evil; for thine is the kingdom, and the power, and the glory, for ever. Amen."*

And the prayer comes to a conclusion on a very powerful note—we need to be delivered from evil. Ours is a devilishly dangerous age. And Jesus taught us to pray, *". . . deliver us from evil . . ."*

This chapter contains a somber message, but I want you to pay attention because, friend, you have an enemy, a real enemy. He has made plans to sabotage your life. The dynamite is in place and the fuse is laid. The match is struck. And you may feel right now that you're sailing along fine on the journey of life, that God is in His heaven, and you don't need to pray. Nothing could be further from the truth.

Satan has always wanted to pull the veil of darkness over his kingdom. But by the aid of the Holy Spirit, I want to rip that veil away and I want us to understand some things about this sinister minister of evil, the devil.

Recognize the Sinister Person of Evil

Now, number one: We need to recognize the sinister person of evil. Verse 13 says, *"Lead us not into temptation, but deliver us from evil . . ."* In the original Greek, it literally says "deliver us from the *evil one.*" He's not just talking about sin, as such. He's talking about Satan. And Jesus taught us to pray that we would be delivered from the evil one—Satan.

The Person of the Evil One

Let's talk about Satan here. Let's talk about his personhood. Satan is a person. He's not a figment of imagination. In 1 Peter 5:8 we read: *"Be sober, be vigilant; because your adversary the devil, as a roaring lion, walketh about, seeking whom he may devour."* You say, "Why am I so important? Why would the devil be after me?" The truth of the matter is you're not that important. Why does Satan want to hurt you? Because God has set His love and His affection on you. Evil persons have always known if you can't get at someone, get at someone that someone loves. Hurt someone that someone loves and you've hurt that someone. Satan cannot get at God directly, but he knows that God has set His affection on you. And so, therefore, he is the bitterest enemy of the people of God. He is your adversary.

He has many aliases, just like every evil person. Let me give you some of the names of this evil one in the Bible. He is called the deceiver. He is called a liar. He is called a murderer. He is called the accuser of the brethren. He is called the tempter. He is called a prince. He is called the destroyer. And here in this model prayer, he is called the evil one. He is intelligent. He is aggressive. He is cunning. And he is destructive. His cleverest ruse is to make people think he doesn't exist, that he is somehow a medieval superstition, that he is just some comical little character dressed in a suit of red underwear with a pitchfork trying to catch somebody bending over. I mean, that's the caricature of our age. So we name football teams "demons." We have "devil's food" cake. We call a car a demon, because to us it's all kind of comical.

And if he can't convince people that he doesn't exist, then the next thing he wants them to think is that he is in hell. He's going to hell, but he's not there yet. He is in our society today.

The apostle Paul said in Ephesians 6:12: *"For we wrestle not against flesh and blood, but against principalities, against powers, against the rulers of the darkness of this world, against spiritual wickedness in high places."* The enemy is not the Democrats. It's not the Republicans. It's not the IRS. It's not your mother-in-law. The battle may show up between flesh and blood, but the problem is not flesh and blood. We have a spiritual enemy. This enemy may have a thousand heads, but he has just one heart. He is a person, a real person.

The Position of the Evil One

I want you to think not only about his person, but think about his position. He has a position of authority. The apostle Paul said, again, in Ephesians 6:12: *"For we wrestle not against flesh and blood* [pay attention to this], *but against principalities, against, powers* [that means authorities], *against the rulers of the darkness of this world, against spiritual wickedness in high places."* We are up against the organized, mobilized, demonized forces of hell. He has a place of great authority. He is the prince of fallen spirits.

There was a rebellion in heaven. And when Satan was cast out of heaven, a third of the angels fell with him, and now he rules a dark domain. In Ephesians 2:2, Paul talks to those who are now saved and reminds them of what they were. He says, *"Wherein in time past ye walked according to the course of this world, according to the prince of the power of the air, the spirit that now worketh in the children of disobedience."* Did you know there's a sense in which all unsaved people are demon-possessed? *". . . the spirit that now worketh in the children of disobedience."*

Satan exercises control, even over the nations of the world. In the UN, in Congress, in Parliament, in all of the various national assemblies, Satan is working. The Bible speaks of how one day we're coming to a battle called the Battle of Armageddon. And the Bible explains how that's going to happen. John, in the Apocalypse, said he saw *"three unclean spirits like frogs come out of the mouth of the dragon, and out of the mouth of the beast, and out of the mouth of the false prophet"* (Rev. 16:3). He explains their agenda in verse 14: *"For they are the spirits of devils, working miracles, going forth unto the kings of the earth and of the whole world, to gather them to the battle of that great day of God Almighty."* Our world is following a demon-led march to Armageddon. And, you wonder why people say such crazy things in national assemblies? Why debates happen as they do? Why can't the people of this world get together? Because there is a devilish spirit that is leading the nations to Armageddon. Therefore, Satan is called the god of this age, spelled with a little "g." Paul said in 2 Corinthians 4:4: *"In whom the god of this world hath blinded the minds of them which believe not . . ."* Don't scold an unsaved man for not seeing the truth. He can't see it. He's blind. The god of this world, Satan, has *"blinded the minds of them which believe not . . ."* He is called the god of this world. Now Satan wants to be like the Most High. He wants to be worshipped. He wants to show himself as a god, the god of this world. What Satan really wants are converts, not casualties.

The Power of the Evil One

We've thought about his personhood. We've thought about his position. Let's think about his power. It is sheer folly to underestimate the power of the devil. Our job as believers is found in Acts 26:18: *"To open their eyes and turn them from darkness to light, and from the power of Satan unto God . . ."* I hear people talk flippantly and lightly about the devil. Now I have no respect for the devil. I have no honor for the devil, but I try not to talk flippantly about the devil. He is a supernatural person. He has supernatural power. He is the supreme dictator over a kingdom of evil.

I suppose my favorite hymn is "A Mighty Fortress Is Our God." And Martin Luther wrote, *"For still our ancient foe doth seek to work us woe. His craft and power are great, and armed with cruel hate, on earth is not his equal."* Don't you sally forth against the devil unless you're armed in the might of Almighty God. You're playing with fire.

The Purpose of the Evil One

Think about his purpose. He is a traitor. He is in open revolt against God. Pride caused him to want to be like the Most High. Did God create the devil? No. God created a perfectly beautiful, majestic angel, but God gave him freedom. God created Satan with perfection, and in that perfection was perfect freedom. And Satan, with his freedom, chose to rebel. And the sin that's in the world has come from the freedom that God gave to this angel called Lucifer, which means "light bearer." Lucifer fell from heaven, and the son of the morning became the father of the night. Lucifer became the devil.

Well, why did God give him such freedom? Why did God give you freedom? Why does God allow sin? Because God must allow a choice. Why must God allow a choice? Because love is the highest good. Jesus was asked in Matthew 22:36–37, "What is the great commandment?" He replied, *"Thou shalt love the Lord thy God with all thy heart, and with all thy soul, and with all thy mind."* Love is the greatest commandment. Now, in order for it to be love, love has to choose. Forced love is a contradiction in terms. There's no such thing as forced love. If you cannot choose not to love, you cannot choose to love. If you cannot choose to be disloyal, you can't choose to be loyal. If God had made us with no ability to choose, God could have no more fellowship with us than I could have with a coffee table. Man has to be able to choose. And so, God gave freedom to the angels, to human beings. God gave us the power to choose. To destroy the power to choose would be in itself evil because it would take away the highest good. God did not create a devil. God created a perfect angel. He revolted against God. Isaiah 14:12–13: *"How art thou fallen from heaven, O Lucifer, son of the morning! How art, how art thou cut down to the ground, which didst weaken the nations! For thou hast said in thine heart, I will ascend into heaven. I will exalt my throne above the stars of God: I will sit also upon the mount of the congregation, in the sides of the north."* One day Satan, infected with pride, said, "I'm too wise, I'm too beautiful to be anything else than God. I will be like God. I will exalt my throne above the stars of God."

What is his purpose? He is in revolt against God; a rebel wanting to ensconce himself as the King of kings and the Lord of lords.

The Plan of the Evil One

Now let's think about his plan. What is his plan? His method is deception. He can do his work no other way. He deceives the nations. He deceives individuals who are lost. And, God help us, many times he deceives the saints. Jesus said in John 8:44 to the unsaved Pharisees, *"You are of your father, the devil, and the lusts of your father ye will do. He was a murderer from the beginning, and abode not in the truth . . ."* Now pay attention to that last phrase. *"He was a murderer from the beginning, and abode not in the truth . . ."* Satan is a murderer. He's a killer. He wants to bring death to youth, to happiness, to joy, to peace, to prosperity. He wants to bring physical death, spiritual death, eternal death. He is a murderer. That is his motive. His method is the lie. *"He was a murderer from the beginning, and abode not in the truth . . ."* The only way the devil can do his dirty, devilish, nefarious work is through deception. Jesus said, *"He was a murderer from the beginning, and abode not in the truth, because there is no truth in him. When he speaketh a lie, he speaketh of his own: for he is a liar, and the father of it."* His plan is to deceive the nations, with a lie. That's the reason Ephesians 6:12 says he is a *"ruler of darkness."*

Now Paul spoke to the church, and he warned the church to be careful in 2 Corinthians 2:11: *"Lest Satan should get an advantage of us: for we are not ignorant of his devices."* We're not ignorant of his devices. Just think of the word *devices*. And then think of 2 Timothy 2:26. Paul says, *"And that they may recover themselves out of the snare of the devil . . ."* Are you beginning to get a picture now? Devices. Snares. Lies. And he's good at it! The most clever lies sound the most like the truth. And there's some truth in every good lie. Somebody said, "A clock that doesn't even run is right twice a day." Satan is a liar.

Now what are some of the things we're up against? Well, we're up against, spiritual wickedness, spiritualism. Do you know what America is full of today? America is full of things like demon worship, necromancy, clairvoyancy, contact with the dead, séances, horoscopes—all of these things. You would think in the twenty-first century those things would be in the tomb of time. But go into any bookstore and go into the religion section. You will find maybe one or two good Bible-based books and the rest will be full of New Age mysticism.

In Deuteronomy 18:9–14, God told His ancient people, *"When thou art come into the land which the LORD thy God giveth thee, thou shalt not learn to do after the abominations of those nations. There shall not be found among you any one that maketh*

> *"The most clever lies sound the most like the truth."*

his son or daughter to pass through the fire [that is, who kills babies], *or that useth divination* [that is, fortune-tellers], *or an observer of times* [that is, somebody who follows after the horoscope] . . ." By the way, are you into astrology? If you are, get out of it. *Astro* means "star"; *logy* means "the word." It's the word of the stars rather than the Word of God. It's one of Satan's tricks. You say, "Well, I just, I just do it for the fun of it." Well, you're doing a little witchcraft for the fun of it. Get out of it! If you've got that stuff in your home, get it out; throw it away.

He goes on, "*. . . or an enchanter, or a witch, or a charmer, or a consulter with familiar spirits, or a wizard, or a necromancer* [that means somebody who, purports to speak to the dead]." People are spending multiplied millions of dollars to talk to departed loved ones. And what they do is to make contact with a demon spirit who imitates their loved ones. And God warns against these things—1 John 4:1: *"Beloved, believe not every spirit, but try* [or test] *the spirits, whether they are of God . . ."* Sometimes people will get into the occult and they'll say to me, "Well, Pastor, there's something to it." I say, "Sure, there's something to it. That's the reason why you need to leave it alone."

I was in the Orlando airport a while back, and I saw one of these demon-possessed young ladies who was a member of a cult. She had a very seductive appearance and manner. I watched her as she would come up to sailors there in the Orlando airport and would pin little American flags on the lapel of their uniforms. And then she would start talking to them, trying to get them to buy this material that she had. It infuriated me. I was hoping she would come talk to me, but since I'm just an old coot and not a young sailor boy, she never even looked in my direction. After a while, I decided I would talk to her, and I moved toward her. I

said, "Young lady, may I say something to you?" She said, "Yes."
I said, "Jesus Christ is Lord." When I said that, she screamed like
a banshee, "Aaaaaaaaaaaa!" filling the airport with a maniacal
scream just at the very mention that Jesus is Lord.

Oh, we're up against demonic powers. But I'll tell you what
else we're up against in our age, and that is drug abuse. The Bible
specifically warns about drug abuse. The Bible says that in the
Great Tribulation drug abuse is going to be rampant. Revelation
9:21: *"Neither repented they of their murders, nor of their sorceries,
nor of their fornication, nor of their thefts."* Four big sins in the
tribulation and one of them is sorcery. Now the word *sorcery* here
comes from a Greek word, *pharmacia*. It's the word we get our
word *pharmacy* from. It has to do with drugs. There's nothing
wrong with dispensing drugs from Walgreens, but he says here,
"sorcery"—*pharmacia*. Thayer's lexicon says that word means "an
enchanter with drugs."

David Wilkerson worked with drug addicts in Hell's Kitchen
in New York City and other places. He said, "I have yet to see anyone who was into demon worship who did not, first of all, open
his mind to spiritual experiences through the use of drugs." Drugs
are Satan's sin, synthetic salvation that leads to everlasting hell.

We're also up against false doctrine. Friend, when you look
for the devil, never fail to look in the pulpit. The apostle Paul
wrote in 1 Timothy 4:1: *"Now the Spirit speaketh expressly, that
in the latter times some shall depart from the faith, giving heed to
seducing spirits and doctrines of devils."* It's an amazing thing. Few

churches today are preaching the old-time religion. Few churches today are standing up for the gospel of our Lord and Savior Jesus Christ. You can write down what you want to believe and how you want to behave, and I can find you a church in any major city in America where you'll be right at home. These are doctrines of demons. The devil occupies the pulpit. He is transformed as an angel of light.

Then consider the corruption, debauchery, violence, and hate—a veritable spirit of anarchy and rebellion—that is in our world today. Where does that come from? From the enemy himself.

All of this is under the point that we need to recognize the sinister person of evil. And if you don't recognize him, you're not going to pray. You're going to waltz out of your house in the morning, thinking it's all right. Everything's fine. But I'm telling you that the dark, devilish influence of the evil one is in the world today.

Realize the Seductive Power of Evil

Not only should you recognize this sinister person of evil, but you need to realize the seductive power of evil. Jesus said, *"Lead us not into temptation . . ."* Well, you say, "Am I tempted? After all, I'm saved." Friend, Jesus is talking to His children. And the Bible says, *"Let him that thinketh he standeth take heed, lest he fall"* (1 Cor. 10:12). And the proud person tempts the devil to tempt him.

You may say, "Well, the devil never bothers me." Well, then you're better than Jesus. Satan tempted Jesus. Friend, if you've never met the devil, it's because you and the devil have been going in the same direction. You're in collusion with him. You turn around, get right with God and begin to live for God, you'll not be in collusion with him; you'll be in collision with him.

Let me ask you a question. Have you ever sinned and asked God to forgive and He did? Now, another question. Have you ever committed the same sin again and asked God to forgive you and He did? How many of you have committed, perhaps, the same thing a hundred times? Five hundred times? One thousand times? Over and over and over again. And you say, "O God, have mercy. God, forgive me." And He does! What a wonderful God we have. *"If we confess our sin, he is faithful and just to forgive us our sins, and to cleanse us from all unrighteousness"* (1 John 1:9). I am grateful that God forgives. But aren't you tired of asking God to forgive you for the same thing? I mean, wouldn't you like to change that? Wouldn't you like to get off the defensive and get on the offensive?

I had a friend who was a linebacker for the Miami Dolphins. They called him Captain Crunch. His name was Mike Kolen.

"If you've never met the devil, it's because you and the devil have been going in the same direction."

After Mike graduated from Auburn University, the coach at that time, Skip Jordan, said, "Mike, will you do some scouting for me?"

Mike said, "Sure, coach. I'd be glad to. What kind of football player are you looking for?"

Coach Jordan said, "Mike, you know, there's a guy—you knock him down and he stays down."

"Coach, we don't want him, do we?"

"No, Mike, we don't want him. But Mike, there's a guy— you knock him down and he gets up. And you knock him down and he stays down."

Mike said, "Well, I don't guess we want him either, do we, coach?"

"No, we don't. But Mike, there a guy—you knock him down and he gets up. You knock him down, he gets up. You knock him down, he gets up. You knock him down, he gets up. You knock him down, he gets up."

Mike said, "That's the guy we want, isn't it, coach?"

"No, I don't want him either. I want you to find that guy that's knocking everybody down."

I'm so grateful that when we get knocked down, we can get up. That's wonderful. We do that by the power of the grace of the Holy Spirit of God. But why is it we keep getting knocked down? I'll tell you why. We have failed to look at what Jesus taught us to pray. Jesus taught us to pray, *"Lead us not into temptation, but deliver us from evil."* Now, we pray, "Father, forgive us our trespasses," and He does. We remember that part of the prayer, but we fail to pray this part of the prayer: *"Lead us not into temptation, but deliver us from evil."*

Now many of us just come and ask God to forgive us, but we don't pray for deliverance. And, therefore, we get right back in the same situation again over and over and over again. And you know what some people do? They try to pray at the end of the day, "Lord, forgive me, forgive me." Well, friend, when is this prayer to be prayed? In the morning. How? What did Jesus teach us? "Give us this day our daily bread." When do you pray for daily bread, just before you go to sleep? I mean, the day is over. This is the prayer that unlocks the morning. And you pray when you get out of bed, "O God, today I want You to keep me from temptation and deliver me from the evil one."

> *"We don't pray for a victory; we pray from the victory. The victory has already been won."*

Satan has a plan. It is very real. And God must lead you and deliver you. Peter, James, and John were with Jesus in the Garden of Gethsemane. After Jesus admonished them to watch and pray, He came back and found them sleeping. Matthew 26:40–41: *"And he cometh unto his disciples and findeth them asleep, and saith unto Peter, What, could ye not watch with me one hour? Watch and pray, that ye enter not into temptation: the spirit indeed is willing, but the flesh is weak."*

Do you know what sin often is? Let me give you a three-part formula: Sin is an undetected weakness, an unexpected opportunity, and an unprotected life. And we sally forth, not realizing the seductive power of evil. You say, "Satan can't get me." Hot shot, he sure can. Jesus taught you to pray, "O Father, don't let me be led into temptation, but deliver me from evil." Satan knows a thousand ways to get you and me. *"And let him that thinketh he standeth take heed, lest he fall"* (1 Cor. 10:12). *"Pride goeth before destruction, and a haughty spirit before a fall"* (Prov. 16:18).

Rely on the Sovereign Protection from Evil

Here's the final thing: Rely on the sovereign protection from evil. I don't want you to focus on the evil; I want you to focus on the glorious kingdom of God. Jesus taught us to pray for deliverance because of this: the kingdom and the power and the glory belong to Him. Now put it all together. *"Father, lead us not into temptation, but deliver us from evil: For thine is the kingdom, and the power, and the glory . . ."* We don't have to be afraid of Satan. I'm not trying to make you afraid of Satan. I'm not afraid of Satan. The Bible says, *"In nothing [be] terrified by your adversaries"* (Phil. 1:28). Why am I not afraid of Satan? Because I know the power and the glory of Almighty God. I know that, *"Greater is he that is in [me] than he that is in the world"* (1 John 4:4).

Now that doesn't mean that I am dispassionate about Satan's power. I know that it is there. But, friend, there are three cords that run through the Bible. If you want to understand the Bible, here are these three cords: There's the dark cord of Satan's revolt and sin. There's the red cord of the blood of redemption. And there's the golden cord of the victorious kingdom of our God. *"For thine is the kingdom, and the power, and the glory . . ."* Satan's back was broken at Calvary. Jesus said, *"Now shall the prince of this world be cast out"* (John 12:31). Jesus said, *"I give you the authority . . . over all the power of the enemy"* (Luke 10:19 NKJV).

"Thine is the kingdom, and the power, and the glory for ever." Satan has no power against you—nada, zip, zero—absolutely none that you cannot break in the power of the Holy Spirit of God. As a matter of fact, you don't pray for a victory; you pray from the victory. The victory has already been won.

You may say, "I'm not afraid of the devil. Well, there's a bigger question: Is the devil afraid of you? He ought to be. The Bible says, "Resist the devil; he will flee from you." So many of us have been beat up by Satan so much, we're like that cat that had his tail stepped on so many times than when somebody would come in the room, he'd just turn around and stick it out and wait for it to be stepped on. You don't think that you can have victory. You hope one day you're going to get to heaven and have the victory.

No! Jesus taught us to pray, *"Lead us not into temptation, but deliver us from evil: For thine is the kingdom . . ."* Jesus is the King; not Satan.

CHAPTER 6

Thine Is the Glory

"The Praise of the Prayer"

"For thine is the kingdom, and the power,
and the glory, for ever. Amen."

—MATTHEW 6:13

Now what is the purpose of prayer? We're coming full circle. Why does God want you to have victory over Satan? Because His is the glory. Why do you pray? To give God the glory. Now notice. *"For thine is . . . the glory . . ."* Pay close attention. When your reason for asking and God's reason for giving are the same, your prayer will be answered. *"For thine is . . . the glory . . ."* Learn to give glory to God. *"Thy kingdom come. Thy will be done on earth, as it is in heaven."*

I love the way this prayer ends because of how it begins: *"Our Father . . ."*

Notice how it ends: *"Thine is the kingdom . . ."* Our Father is the King.

When I was getting ready to go off to college, my dad said, "Adrian, I'm happy you're going to college. I wish I could pay your way through college, but I can't." I said, "That's all right, Dad. God's called me to preach, and He's going to see me through." And He did! But my heavenly Father will never have to say to me, "Adrian, there's something I'd like to do for you, but I just can't." Friend, our Father is a King. We have the sympathy of a Father and the sovereignty of a King. *"Our Father . . ." "Thine is the kingdom, and the power, and the glory for ever."* This prayer begins with praise. It ends with praise. And if you run out of things to pray for, just begin to praise and you'll have an ocean to swim in.

Here are five very practical, but wonderful reasons for learning to praise the Lord. And, if you'll do it, I'll guarantee it will change your life.

Praise Glorifies Our God

Psalm 147:1 says: *"Praise ye the LORD: for it is good to sing praises unto our God; for it is pleasant"*—now, watch this—*"and praise is comely."* What that literally means is that praise is appropriate; it is the appropriate thing to praise God. If you'll study the created universe, you'll find out that everything that God has created has been created to bring Him glory.

Psalm 145:10 says: *"All thy works shall praise thee, O LORD; and thy saints shall bless thee."* Psalm 148:1–5: *"Praise ye the LORD. Praise ye the LORD from the heavens: praise him in the heights. Praise . . . him, all his angels: praise ye him, all his hosts. Praise . . . him, sun and moon: praise him, all ye stars of light. Praise him, ye heavens of heavens, and ye waters that be above the heavens. Let them praise the name of the LORD: for he commanded, and they were created."* The entire universe of things, living and non-living, is to be one great, grand chorus and paean of

> *"We have the sympathy of a Father and the sovereignty of a King."*

praise to our great God. Do you know what the highest occupation of the angels is? It is praising God.

Now, why does praise glorify God? Well, the very word *worship*, comes from the Old English *worth-ship*. The way you praise God tells me what you think of God. Very frankly, the way you praise God tells me what God is worth to you; it tells God what He is worth to you. Praise glorifies God. He is worthy of our praise.

Have you ever heard a person take God's name in vain in some profane curse? Doesn't that just rip your heart out? It grieves me to hear people use profanity, and I'll tell you why: because profanity degrades God. Sometimes a person will curse, and you remonstrate with them about it; and they say, "Well, I didn't mean anything by it." I say, "Well, that makes it doubly worse—that you could take the name of the thrice holy God of Israel and not mean anything by it." You see, profanity degrades God; praise glorifies God. That's the first reason: praise glorifies our God.

Praise Heals Our Hurts

Not only does praise glorify our God, but praise heals our hurts. *"The LORD doth build up Jerusalem: he gathereth together the outcasts of Israel"*—that is, those who are broken, and wounded, and bruised, and bleeding. He just puts His arms around them—*"He healeth the broken in heart, and bindeth up their wounds"* (Ps. 147:2–3).

Now, let me tell you what God gave to you: God gave you a body, a soul, and a spirit. Each one has a function. The function of the body is obvious: the body is the spacesuit we wear so we can live on planet Earth and we can express ourselves. The soul is the mind, the emotion, and the will that lives inside of this body that motivates this body, that drives this body, and gives it direction. The spirit is the organ of praise created to praise God, to know God, to reverence God. You are body, soul, and spirit.

One particular Sunday afternoon I was sitting in my recliner chair. I had already preached three times that morning and made a visit after lunch. And, I got in that chair, and, frankly, it felt good and my body liked it. When it was time to go back to church for the evening service, my body said, "I want to stay in this chair." That's what my body said. I also need to mention that it was Super Bowl Sunday and the game was coming on soon. My soul said, "I want to watch the Super Bowl." But my spirit said, "I want to go to church and worship God." Now, the spirit is the organ of praise, and my spirit said to soul, "Soul, we're going to church." And, my soul said to my body, "Get up!" And that's the way it ought to be.

There's a chain of command. Now, when a man is overridden by his soul, he's carnal. When he's overridden by his body, he's not worth shooting. And, some are actually slaves to their body. But, my dear friend, the spirit is to have control. And the function of your spirit is to praise. And, dear friend, the highest function that the human spirit can attain is to praise God. That's why God created you.

Now, I said that praise heals our hurts. Did you know that we have a lot of Christians in mental institutions? We have Christians—some of them taking tranquilizers like salted peanuts. They have mental and nervous disorders. Now, sometimes there are reasons for that, and nobody is to be blamed for it. There, indeed, are chemical imbalances. There are physiological reasons. And, I want to tell you something, friend: proper praise could almost put some psychiatrists out of business. I'm telling you the truth. A lot of our mental and nervous disorders would disappear if we learned how to praise.

And why is that? Why does praise not only glorify God and heal our hurts as well? *"He healeth the broken in heart and [He] bindeth up their wounds"* (Ps. 147:3). Why? Well, I'll tell you what carnality is and what most of our mental disorders are caused by: it is an over-occupation with our personal egos. We get self-centered. And, when one gets extremely self-centered, do you know what happens? Do you know what the next step of being extremely self-centered is? It's to be defensive. A self-centered person is always a defensive person; he's always defending himself. And do you know what happens when a person gets overly defensive? He becomes hostile. In order to defend himself, he feels like he has to be hostile toward you. And do you know what happens when a person gets hostile? He becomes aggressive. You see, anybody who is self-centered rather than God-centered is self-destructive.

In Luke 9:24, Jesus said, *"Whosoever will save his life shall lose it: but whosoever will lose his life for my sake, the same shall save it."* Do you want to save your life? Well, dear friend, just lose it. Give yourself to God in praise, and you're going to find out that, rather than being self-centered and defensive and hostile and aggressive, that the spiritual juices are going to begin to flow in your heart. You see, you cannot genuinely praise God without relinquishing that self-centeredness. There's no way that you can do it. When praise becomes a way of life, the infinitely lovely God becomes the center of your self—the center of your being—rather than your bankrupt self.

There is nothing so empty as a self-centered life. There is nothing so centered as a self-emptied life. And we need to learn to praise God. It just heals our hearts. You can't praise and sulk at the same time. Praise and irritation cannot coexist. Praise and pride cannot live together. In Isaiah 61:3, the Bible says that God has given us *"the garment of praise for the spirit of heaviness."* And, you want to cast off that spirit of heaviness? Put on the garment of praise. What does praise do? Number one: it glorifies God. Number two: it heals our hurts. Friend, praise will do more for you than any psychiatrist or psychologist can do for you. I'm not against these people. We have some lovely people in our church who do a wonderful job helping people. But they, too, would say, "Praise is a marvelous, wonderful tool for healing the human spirit."

Praise Fortifies Our Faith

Not only does praise glorify God, not only does praise heal our hurts, but praise fortifies our faith. Now, without faith it is impossible to please God. Speaking of God, Psalm 147:4 says:

"He telleth the number of the stars"—have you ever thought about how many billions and quadzillions of stars are out there? There are innumerable stars, yet God knows every one of them—*"he [calls] them all by their names."* Did you know that every star in this stellar universe has a name that God has given it? Every one of them. The psalmist continues—*"Great is our Lord, and of great power: his understanding is infinite. The LORD lifteth up the meek: [and] he casteth the wicked down to the ground"* (Ps. 147:4–6).

Now, what does praise do? Praise reminds you one more time, dear friend, that "this is my Father's world." I mean, the God that runs this universe is my personal heavenly Father. And not a blade of grass moves without His permission. Not a speck of dust blows around without His permission. You see, praise is a form of faith. Praise is worry turned inside out. It's just simply a way of saying, "God is over all, and no matter what my problem is, God is greater." And, the psalmist here speaks of the greatness of God and tells how He handles this mighty universe. And friend, if He can number the stars, He can take care of your problems—He can. Praise glorifies God—it glorifies our God. It heals our hurts. It fortifies our faith.

Praise Tells Our Thanksgiving

I'll tell you something else it does: it tells our thanksgiving. You can tell a thankful man by the way he praises. Psalm 147:7–9: *"Sing unto the LORD with thanksgiving; sing praise upon the harp unto our God: Who covereth the heaven with clouds, who prepareth rain for the earth, who maketh grass to grow upon the mountains. He giveth to the beast his food, and to the young ravens which cry."* Oh, how good God is!

Now, how can you tell me that you are thankful to God and you don't praise God? I think the meanest thing on this earth is an unthankful man. Oh, we think we have things to complain about. I heard about a man who went to the grocery store with a shopping bag full of money and came home with a billfold full of groceries. Maybe you can identify with that. But, before you complain too much, just think how

"Praise is worry turned inside out."

God has blessed America. And do you know why God has blessed America? Not because Americans are bigger, smarter; not because our land is more fertile. We enjoy God's blessings here in America because we have followed the Judeo-Christian ethic that comes directly from the Word of God.

I was reading a while back that in Russia a man has to work one hour to earn a loaf of bread. Do you know how long a man has to work in America, on average, to earn a loaf of bread? Six minutes. A Russian works one hour and eleven minutes for a quart of milk. An American works nine minutes for a quart of milk. For a suit of clothes, a Russian must work 583 hours to get one suit of clothes. An American—38 hours for a fine suit of clothes. A cotton dress in Russia—you'd work 225 hours. In America, you work four hours for that dress. Eighty-five percent of the people in the world don't have enough to eat. Most Americans have bread enough and to spare.

"Well," you say, "I don't have everything I need." That's not the important thing, dear friend. Do you appreciate what you do have? I'd rather appreciate the things I do have than to have the things I don't appreciate. Thank God for His goodness to us. God is good. And friend, if you can't be thankful for what you've received, be thankful for what you've escaped. Thank God you don't get what you deserve. I'm telling you that God is good. And I'll see not only your attitude of your worth of God, but the thankful spirit that you have by the way you praise. Praise glorifies our God. Praise heals our hurts. Praise tells our thanksgiving.

Praise Protects Our Peace

I'll tell you what else praise does: praise protects our peace. In Psalm 147:10–14, the Bible says, *"He delighteth not in the strength of the horse: he taketh not pleasure in the legs of a man. The Lord taketh pleasure in them that fear him, in those that hope in his mercy. Praise the Lord, O Jerusalem; praise thy God, O Zion. For he hath strengthened the bars of thy gates; he hath blessed thy children within thee. He maketh peace in thy borders."* Praise protects our peace.

Now, when he talks about horses and the legs of a man, what he's saying is that God is not impressed with our armaments. Star Wars or whatever else is not going to protect America. As I've said before, America's biggest threat is God, and its only hope is God. We'd better learn that. I mean, without God we're going down. You can see in the Bible over and over again where people would praise the Lord and God would give them peace. When this nation begins to praise God, God's going to give us peace within our borders.

There is a marvelous story in 2 Chronicles 20. The armies of the Moabites and the Ammonites in Mount Seir had come against Judah and Jerusalem. King Jehoshaphat said, "God, what shall we do?" And God said, "You begin to praise. You get your army, and you put the praises out there. You send the troops into the battle praising the Lord." The Bible says when Judah—and the word *Judah* means "praise"—began to praise, God sent an ambush against the enemies of God.

Now why did God instruct King Jehoshaphat to do that? I'll tell you why: Judah was the messianic tribe. That is, Jesus is a descendant of the tribe of Judah. Revelation 5:5 calls Him "the Lion of the tribe of Judah." And Satan had inspired and motivated this confederacy of nations to destroy Judah through whom the Savior was to come. And so, when we know the will of God, when we see the plan of God, when we begin to praise the works of God, God moves in. If you're ever up against the devil, learn to praise, and I'll tell you why: because God inhabits the praise of His people. Psalm 22:3: *"O thou that inhabitest the praises of Israel."* Do you want to know what God's address is? Where does God live? It's praise; that's where God lives. Now, you say, "Well, God is always present, isn't He?" Oh, yes, He is omnipresent, but He is dynamically present when people praise. And, just as God moves into praise, Satan is allergic to praise. Wherever there is massive, triumphant praise, Satan is paralyzed, Satan is bound, and Satan is banished.

These are five wonderful reasons we ought to praise the Lord: praise glorifies our God; praise heals our hurts; praise fortifies our faith; praise tells our thanks, and praise protects our peace.

Praise needs not to be something that you do once in a while; praise needs to be the permanent pattern of your heart. Psalm 57:7 says, *"My heart is fixed, O God, my heart is fixed: I will sing and give praise."* Don't praise just simply by emotion, by whim. Just say, "I've made up my mind. My heart is fixed. I'll do it." We praise by principle and not by impulse. We praise no matter what happens. Praise Him in the good times; praise Him in the bad. Praise Him in the sunshine; praise Him in the rain. Praise Him through sorrow; praise Him in times of happiness. *"I will bless the Lord at all times: his praise shall continually be in my mouth."* (Ps. 34:1).

CHAPTER 7

Ask, Seek, Knock

"The Promise of the Prayer"

"Ask, and it shall be given you; seek, and ye shall find;
knock, and it shall be opened unto you."

—MATTHEW 7:7

The disciples asked Jesus to teach them to pray, and He gave them that model prayer. First of all, He talked about the person of the prayer: *"Our Father, which art in heaven . . ."* He talked about the priority of the prayer: *"Thy kingdom come. Thy will be done . . ."* He talked about the provision of the prayer:

"Give us this day our daily bread." He talked about the pardon of the prayer: *"And forgive us our debts, as we forgive our debtors."* He talked about the protection of the prayer: *"Lead us not into temptation, but deliver us from evil . . ."* He talked about the praise of the prayer: *"For thine is the kingdom, the power, and the glory for ever."*

In the very next chapter, Matthew 7:7–11, Jesus adds this postscript—what I call the promise of the prayer: *"Ask, and it shall be given you; seek, and ye shall find; knock, and it shall be opened unto you: For every one that asketh receiveth; and he that seeketh findeth; and to him that knocketh it shall be opened. Or what man is there of you, whom if his son ask bread, will he give him a stone? Or if he ask a fish, will he give him a serpent? If ye then, being evil, know how to give good gifts unto your children, how much more shall your Father which is in heaven give good things to them that ask him?"*

Three words. Never forget them. Ask, seek, knock. A–S–K. Do you want to get your prayers answered? That's the way to do it. These are three little words, but a small key can open a very big door to a very vast room full of rich treasures. We need to learn how to ask. We need to learn how to seek. And we need to learn how to knock if we're going to take this lesson in prayer that our Lord gave to us and live it out day to day.

When We Ask, We Express Desire

Our Lord says, "*What things soever ye desire when you pray, believe that you receive them, and ye shall have them*" (Mark 11:24). Do you know what the greatest problem in prayer with most of us is? We just don't do it. The greatest problem is not unanswered prayer; it is unoffered prayer. Our Lord taught us to ask. James 4:2:"*Ye have not, because ye ask not.*"

Prayer begins with asking. We ask. Did you know our Lord has commanded us to pray? Luke 18:1: "*Then He spoke a parable to them, that men always ought to pray and not lose heart*" (NKJV). Again, the apostle Paul, in Philippians 4:6, says, "*In everything by prayer and supplication, with thanksgiving, let your requests be made known to God*" (NKJV).

Lack of prayer is not just merely missing a blessing; it is disobedience. It's high treason against heaven's King. There is no substitute for prayer. If you lose a leg, you can get an artificial leg. If

> "*The greatest problem is not unanswered prayer; it is unoffered prayer.*"

you don't have a telephone, you can use email. If you don't have email, you can use snail mail. You can get the message out some way. Seriously, friend, you can find a substitute for some things. There is no substitute for prayer. Not eloquence, not energy, not enthusiasm, not intellect, not intention.

Most people I know would readily agree with this statement: "God answers prayer." But do we really believe it? If we really believe that God answers prayer, and we don't pray, then we're fools. The cause of our powerlessness is our prayerlessness. I believe with all of my heart the greatest untapped resource in the universe is prayer. We don't have a need but what proper prayer would supply it. We don't have a sin but what proper prayer would have avoided it. Prayer can do anything that God can do—and God can do anything!

We already asked why does God want us to pray? Why doesn't God just do it? He knows what we have need of before we ask Him. Remember, I told you we don't pray to instruct God. Who can tell God what to do? We don't pray to inform God. Who can tell Him anything He doesn't know? We certainly don't pray to impress God. How are you going to impress the Almighty? We pray to invite God to work in our hearts and in our lives. What a delight prayer is. *"Delight yourself in the LORD, and He will give you the desires of your heart"* (Ps. 37:4 NKJV). Prayer develops you. You grow in prayer. That's the reason Jesus gave this promise in John 15:7: *"If ye abide in me, and my words abide in you, ye shall ask what ye will, and it shall be done unto you."* You see, prayer leads us to abide. God wants us to abide. He doesn't want us to be independent of Him. If He were to do things for us without our asking Him, then we would never abide. But we need to abide in Him, just as a vine does a branch.

Sometimes you may wonder whether a thing is right for you or wrong for you. A good test about anything is, can you ask God for it? If you can't ask God for it, you don't have any business wanting it. You have no right to desire anything that you cannot ask God for. And if you desire it, you ought to be able to pray about it. No matter how big or how small, you ought to be able to come to God and ask God for it.

Have you ever prayed for a parking place? That's legitimate. You can pray for anything. Prayer ought to be as natural as breathing. That's what it means to pray without ceasing. It doesn't mean that you're constantly mumbling, but your heart is always in tune with God; you're turning to Him and looking to Him. There is nothing too big or nothing too small.

If you have a desire, ask God. What if you have a wrong desire? Tell Him about that. Say, "Lord, I want something that I ought not to want. Fix my wanter."

Let me let you in on a secret. Satan cannot keep God from answering your prayer, so he keeps you from asking. Our Lord Jesus Christ said, *"Ask, and you shall receive."* But it doesn't end there.

When We Seek, We Explore Direction

Not only when we ask do we express desire, but He also says seek. *"Seek, and ye shall find . . ."* Desire and direction need to come together. You see, it's important that our asking be linked with seeking because sometimes we may be asking for things that are not God's will.

Let me tell you how real prayer works. The Bible says, *"For of Him, and through Him, and to Him are all things"* (Rom. 11:36 NKJV). That's the divine triangle. That's how prayer works. That's how all the Christian life works.

Now here's another secret. The prayer that gets to heaven is the prayer that starts in heaven. We close the circuit. That's all we do. Let me give you a definition of prayer. Prayer is the Holy Spirit finding a desire in the heart of the Father, putting that desire into our heart, and then sending it back to heaven in the power of the cross.

So we need to seek. We need to find out what is the mind of the Spirit. We need to understand the will of God. So, yes, ask. But sometimes we don't know what to ask for. So we need to seek until we find the right answer.

Sometime ago, I was invited to go to a breakfast meeting in downtown Memphis, Tennessee. A fellow pastor was going to come by and pick me up, and I was going to take Joyce with me. The meeting started early—at seven o'clock. And it took quite a time to get to downtown Memphis from where we lived. So Joyce and I got dressed and we were waiting for our man to come and pick us up. And he didn't show. It dawned on me that we were supposed to meet him downtown, and there's no way we could get there now in time for this meeting. I could tell you exactly the place where I was in our kitchen, and I stopped. I was standing in front of the refrigerator and I prayed. No one else was around, so I prayed out loud. And, by the way, it's good to pray out loud; you can hear yourself and keep your mind clear. And I prayed out loud. I said, "Father, I can't go to that breakfast. What do You want me to do?" I felt a distinct impression in my heart: "Take Joyce to breakfast." Now, again, I don't normally pray about where I'm going to go to breakfast or what I should do at that time. I just make up my mind and do it. But I prayed. I felt impressed to pray.

And the Holy Spirit said, "Take Joyce to breakfast." Well, you say that's a kind of no-brainer. You're all dressed and you haven't had breakfast yet. But I said, "Lord, where should I take her to breakfast?" I don't normally pray about where I'm going to go to breakfast, but I felt this distinct leadership of the Lord: "Take her to the Holiday Inn at Poplar and I-240." There's not a Holiday Inn there today. It's now something else. But at one time, in Memphis, there was a Holiday Inn at Poplar and I-240. Now, if you're with Holiday Inn, I'm sorry, but frankly, the Holiday Inn would not be my first choice for breakfast. But I prayed. And the Lord said to me, as far as I know, "Take Joyce to breakfast to the Holiday Inn." Not just any. He told me the exact one to go to. So I said, "Joyce, we're going to the Holiday Inn, I-240 and Poplar, for breakfast."

We got in our car and went. They took us in and put us right in front of a plate-glass window so the cars that were parking would pull up and look right in the window at us. We're sitting there at breakfast. A man parks his car, gets out, and comes in, and says, "I cannot believe this." He said, "You are the one man in all this city that I need to talk to. It's Saturday. Your phone number is unlisted. I have no way of finding you. You hold the key to my future, the one man in this whole city, and there you are right there." And he told me a story about trouble in his family.

His wife was ready to leave him. And when I heard his story, I understood why. And he said, "I need God's mercy. I need God's help. I need my wife to change her mind. I love her. You are the only man that she trusts. She's been listening to you preach. Would you possibly, could you please talk with my wife?" I said, "I will, sir. You get her and bring her by my house." That couple came to my house. In my little home study they sat down with me and gave their hearts to Jesus. And God put that home back together right there with the grace of God. Today, that's one of the finest families in our church! That man and his wife are pristine, glorious, wonderful Christians, and have been so for many, many years.

Now I want to ask you a question: Do you think it was by happenstance that I happened to go to the Holiday Inn and we sat right in front of that window at that moment when a man was desperately seeking God, wanting God? You know, when we seek, God leads. The point I'm trying to say is that the prayer that gets to heaven is the prayer that starts in heaven. What we do is close the circuit when we're walking in the Spirit.

Many times we don't get our prayers answered because we don't seek. We are to seek, first of all, the purpose of God. Ask, "Lord, what is Your purpose? What are You up to?" Many times our prayers are selfish in their motivation. He says, *"You ask and do not receive because you ask amiss"* (James 4:3). You ask wrongly. Sometimes we're asking for things that God is not going to give, and we need to seek and to find His will. Sometimes it's not the purpose of God that we need to seek; sometimes it's the very presence of God. James 4:8 says, *"Draw nigh to God, and he will draw nigh unto you."* Sometimes we need to keep seeking until God is real to us. And the gift without the giver is bare. Sometimes our prayers are too mechanical. They're too cold-hearted. God does business with those who mean business and seek His presence. Sometimes it's the power of God that we need to seek, and we're asking for the right thing, but God is working in us and He's saying, "Seek Me, not just My hand. Seek My face and then you'll see My hand."

God called me to preach when I was in high school. I didn't know much about preaching. I didn't come from a line of preachers. I didn't know theology. I'd not been a scholar in high school. I had a good enough mind that I could get by without studying, and I took advantage of it. But God called me to preach. And I had enough sense to know that I needed the power of God in my life.

I went out one summer night under the Florida skies, a starlit night. Walked up and down on the football field where I had practiced. Nobody else was out there. By myself. Walked up and down and prayed and said, "O God, I want You, and I want You to use me. O God, I am seeking You. I want You, God. I want You to use me." And I stopped walking and I got on my knees out there in the middle of that field at night by myself, and I said, "Lord, I want You to use me. Please, Lord, use me." And that didn't seem humble enough, so I laid down on the grass and put my face down before the Lord, spread my hands out, and I said, "O God, I humble myself before You. I want You to use me." And that didn't seem enough. And I took my finger and I made a hole in the dirt and I put my nose down in that hole till the dirt came up my nostrils, and I said, "God, I am as low as I know how to get. I want You to use me."

And God moved into my life. I didn't know theology. I didn't understand all of the things that I know now about the Holy Spirit of God. But God did something in my heart and in my life because I learned not just to seek His hand, but to seek His face, to seek Him.

And that's what prayer is all about. Not just merely to ask for desires, but to seek for direction, to seek God. Many times our prayers don't seem to be answered right away. Maybe it's the purpose of God that we need to seek. Maybe it's the presence of God we need to seek. Maybe it's the power of God that we need to seek.

When We Knock, We Exercise Determination

When we ask, we express desire. When we seek, then we explore direction. But when we knock, we exercise determination. God says we're to ask. We're to seek. And we're to knock. Friend, we need our desires, our direction, and our determination all to line up when we pray. Sometimes when we pray, there are some barriers that need to be overcome. Sometimes there seem to be some closed doors that need to be opened.

In the Greek language, this verse—that tells us to ask, seek, and knock—is in the present tense, and it implies continuous action. it literally says, "Keep on asking, keep on seeking, keep on knocking." It speaks of determination; it speaks of persistence.

Sometimes answers to prayer come immediately and direct. We ask, and just like that, God gives the answer. I've had Him do that in incredible ways. I've had Him heal me instantaneously. I woke up with an excruciating pain, and I said, "O God, in the name of Jesus, heal me," and it was gone. Some might say, "Coincidence." Well, they can think what they want, and I'll think what I want.

I was on my way to speak one time on a Sunday afternoon on a lonely Florida highway, and my car stopped running. It didn't slow down; it just stopped. I thought, *Now what is this?* I got out. Opened the hood. Everything looked fine to me. I got back in. I turned the key. It wouldn't start. It was just completely dead. I said, "Well, Lord, send somebody along."

Nobody came. I said, "Lord, if You're the great physician, You're the great mechanic. I want You to heal my car." You might be thinking, *That's so silly*, but let me tell you what happened. I laid my hand on the hood of that car, and I said, "Lord Jesus, I want You to fix this car. Thank You." Got in. *Brooooooooom*. And off I went. And I never took it in the shop. I don't know what was wrong with it. God knew. God fixed it. Whether you believe in God healing cars or not, I do. Sometimes the answer to prayer is direct like that.

Sometimes the answer to prayer is not direct; it's different. You ask God for one thing and God gives you something better. Has that ever happened to you? The Bible says, "*We do not know what we should pray for as we ought, but the Spirit Himself makes intercession for us with groanings which cannot be uttered*" (Rom. 8:26 NKJV).

There was a man who was unfaithful to my daughter. He married her and then took up with another woman. Joyce and I stained heaven with our prayers. My daughter was willing to forgive and restore, but this man was enamored with his sin. And I prayed and I prayed and I prayed, and I said, "Lord, those two little girls need their daddy. Lord, that's supposed to be a holy home. O God, put it back together. Please, God, please change that man, Lord, change that man. Lord, change that man." I told Him. I even shouted at God; not in disrespect. I shouted. I said, "God, how can You allow this?" And I just kept on asking, kept on seeking, kept on knocking. The Lord said to me,

"Adrian, you're asking Me to do something that I'm not going to do. You're asking Me to change a man's heart without his permission. I'm not going to do that. He's a man. I gave him a choice. I will help him. I will restore him. I will give him everything he needs, but I will not force his will. You're asking out of My will, Adrian." But He said, "Adrian, those two girls that you're concerned about, I'm going to take care of those two girls. Don't you worry about it." I could not begin to tell you the glorious things God has done in my daughter's life and the life of those two girls. I give Him the praise and the honor and the glory. Sometimes the answer is direct. Sometimes the answer is different.

Sometimes the answer is not different, but it is delayed. Sometimes we don't get that immediate answer. When the answer is delayed, Jesus instructs us to keep knocking. Luke 11:5–10: *"And he said unto them, Which of you shall have a friend, and shall go unto him at midnight and say unto him, Friend, lend me three loaves; For a friend of mine in his journey is come to me, and I have nothing to set before him? And he from within shall answer and say, Trouble me not: the door is shut, and my children are with me in bed . . ."* Here's a man at the door—somebody who comes by on a journey. And in Middle Eastern hospitality, you know what it is? He's got to feed him. There are no 7-Elevens. And so the neighbor next door has bread. The man at the door doesn't have bread, and he's going over there and knocking. Jesus says, "*. . . knock and it shall be opened unto you.*" He's knocking. The man inside says, "Hey, don't trouble me. The door is shut." They had complicated locks in those days. Then he says, *". . . and my children are with me in bed: I cannot rise and give thee."*

In the Middle East, many times they keep animals under the house. And if the animals wake up, the dogs start barking, the children start crying. You know what it's like in the middle of the night. He says, "Hey, hey, man, go away, go away. We're already in bed; get out of here." And Jesus goes on with the parable and says, *"I say unto you, Though he will not rise and give him, because he is his friend, yet because of his importunity* [that means because of his persistence], *he will rise and give him as many as he needeth. As I say unto you Ask, and it shall be given you; seek, and ye shall find; knock, and it shall be opened unto you. For every one that asketh receiveth; and he that seeketh findeth; and to him that knocketh* [literally "to him that keeps on knocking"] *it shall be opened."* The man says, *"Shhhh*, go away. You're going to wake up the baby. And my wife—listen. If you wake up that baby—there, you're going to start the dog barking. Go away." *Knock knock knock.* "I said, go away." *Knock knock knock.* "I said, go away." *Knock knock knock.* And he just keeps on knocking! And the man says, "Oh good night! We'll never get rid of this guy. Martha, is there any bread in the house? Come, give him the bread. Take this bread and go!"

Now Jesus is not like that neighbor. That's not the point. The point that our Lord is making is importunity, persistence. Again, I want to tell you that God does business with those that mean business.

In Luke 18:1, Jesus told His disciples that *"men ought always to pray, and not to faint."* Then, to illustrate this principle of persistence, Jesus told a parable about an unjust judge and a widow. Some shyster had mistreated this widow, and the judge didn't seem to care. And the widow just kept on pestering him and pestering him and pestering him until finally the judge, in order to get her out of his hair, adjudicated her case rightly. Now our Lord is not saying that the Father in heaven is unjust, but He's saying, "You see their persistence."

There was a Syro-Phoenician woman. The Phoenicians were pagans. And this woman had a daughter who was demon-possessed. Jesus was in that area, and this woman came to Him and said, "Jesus, I need You. My daughter is possessed with a demon." Jesus said to her, "I don't have anything to do with you. You're a Gentile. I've come to the lost sheep of the house of Israel. I've come to the Jews. Why, I'm not going to take the children's bread and give it to dogs." You can hardly imagine Jesus speaking that way. "It's not fitting to take bread from the table and give it to the dogs."

What would you have done if Jesus talked to you that way? You would say, "Some religious leader he is. So long! I'll go seek something else." Jesus said, "I'm not going to take the children's bread and give it to dogs. That's not right. That's not fitting." You know what she said? She said, "Lord, You're exactly right." But then she said, "But even the dogs get the crumbs that fall from the table." And she didn't use the same word for dog that He used. He used the dog that meant household pet. She used the word that meant mangy, yellow, back alley dog. She took it down a step lower, and she said, "Lord, yes, that's right. I don't deserve anything. But, O God, I have a need."

Jesus' heart broke. He wasn't being cruel. He was just getting that woman to come to this place of persistence where she would not take no for an answer. And Jesus said, "O woman, great is your faith, great is your faith." And the Master did for her what He wanted.

You know, sometimes it seems like God doesn't want to answer our prayers, like that man in bed doesn't want to get up, like that judge who doesn't want to answer the prayer, like this Syro-Phoenician woman, like Jacob when he was wrestling with the angel of the Lord. And the angel said, "Let me go." Now, wait a minute. No angel has to say to a mortal, "Let me go." This was the angel of Jehovah. The angel was saying, "Let me go," but then not trying all that hard to get away. Friend, that fight was fixed. The angel was just waiting for Jacob to prevail. And finally Jacob said, "I will not let thee go unless you bless me." At that moment, Jacob, which means "con artist" became Israel, which means "a prince with God."

"God does business with those that mean business."

On the road to Emmaus, those disciples were walking along after the resurrection. Jesus, in His resurrected form, walked along with them, opened to them the Scriptures, and showed them in all the Scriptures the things concerning Himself. How would you like to have a tape recording of that? Walking along, opening the Bible. And then the Bible says that, *"He made as if he would have gone further"* (Luke 24:28). That is, "See you later." But they said, "Oh, no, no, no, no, no, no. Don't you go. You stay and eat with us." Now He didn't really want to go further, but He wanted them to want Him.

What I'm trying to say is that when you ask, you express desire. When you seek, you explore direction. You don't always know. And when you knock, you show determination. You exert determination. You ask and you ask and you ask. Ask, seek, and knock.

That brings up a real question. How long should we ask? When do we stop knocking? Perhaps we're knocking and the answer doesn't come. Well, there are three ways for you to know when to stop. First of all, if you have the answer, you can just start praising—when you have the answer in your hand. When my car started, man, I just had a fit! Shouted all over the highway! Praise the Lord! I didn't ask Him anymore because I had what I wanted.

Now, maybe you don't have the answer in your hand; maybe you have the answer in your heart. When God spoke to me about those two grandbabies, He said, "Adrian, I'm going to take care of those." I didn't have the answer in my hand. *I* did not know how He was going to do it, but *He* did, and I had the answer in my heart. And I didn't ask Him anymore about that. I had the assurance that I had received the thing.

There's a third time when you should stop asking, and that's when God says no. Did you know *no* is an answer to prayer? Sometimes He just says no. Mrs. Billy Graham said, "If God had not said no to me, I would have married the wrong man on three different occasions." Sometimes God just says no.

The apostle Paul had a thorn in the flesh. Three times he asked God to take it away from him, and God did not give him the answer to his prayer, as such. He did not take away the thorn, but He gave Paul that added grace, and said, *"My strength is made perfect in weakness"* (2 Cor. 12:9). Paul didn't say, "What can't be cured must be endured." He said, "What can't be cured will be enjoyed." He said, "All right. I will glory in my infirmity." That's faith, isn't it?

So there comes a time when you get the answer. You stop asking. Or when you have the answer in your heart, you stop asking. Or when God just says, "No, that's not My will." But if God doesn't give you then what you asked for, He will give you something better than you asked for.

In Matthew 7:9–11, Jesus illustrates it a little bit more: *"Or what man is there of you, whom, if ye, if his son ask bread, will he give him a stone? Or if he ask a fish, will he give him a serpent? If ye then, being evil, know how to give good gifts unto your children, how much more shall your Father which is in heaven give good things to them that ask him?"*

Do you know why prayer is so important? First of all, because God is good. He says, "If you evil people can take care of your children, how much more would a God, a good God do it?" And not only is God good, but God is wise. If you ask for a fish, He's not going to give you a stone. If you ask for bread, He's not going to give you a serpent. God is too wise to give you something that is wrong. God is good. God is wise. And God is able, for He says, "Your Father who is in heaven . . ." He is a great and mighty God. We have a Father who loves us, and we have a King who can answer us. We have sympathy and sovereignty.

I hope that you'll take the words of Matthew 7:7–8, put them to memory, and begin to ask, to seek, and to knock and find out that our God is a prayer-answering God who has said, *"Call upon Me, and I will answer thee, and show thee great and mighty things which thou knowest not"* (Jer. 33:3).

Would you ask the Lord to teach you to pray? Not teach you *how* to pray, but to teach you to pray. This is a constant battle. Sidlow Baxter was a great Bible teacher. He's in heaven now. But one time he spoke at our church. And he said that the devil must surely say to his cohorts, to his demons, concerning us, "Keep them from praying. Keep them from praying. Because if you can keep them from praying, we can beat them every time. But if they pray, they will beat us every time."